If you are tired of struggle and surviva[l] this book will open the door and se[t] McNeal hits the nail right on the hea[d] gets results. Many consultants charge t... _____ __ _____tion. *Caught Between a Dream and a Job* may be the best investment you have ever made. Read it today!

—Dr. Robert Anthony
Behavioral psychologist, NLP practitioner, and best-selling author

Delatorro McNeal is a young man on a mission...a mission to change the world! And that is exactly what he is doing! If you are serious about success, then this book is a must-read! Read it, then reread it. It will inspire you and empower you to get past your job and get into living your dreams at the highest level! I highly recommend this book!

—Willie Jolley
Best-selling author of *It Only Takes a Minute to Change Your Life*

Ambition is the springboard for success, but hard work and confidence power it forward. Delatorro does a marvelous job of outlining the steps along this path that can guide you to your dreams.

—Nido Qubein
President, High Point University
Chairman, Great Harvest Bread Co.

Delatorro has nailed it! This book is success on steroids! You will be riveted to these pages as you discover the timeless truth that success comes by choice, not chance! Del's powerful personality and writing style will hold your mind captive as his instruction methodically reconstructs the steps of your home, relationships, career, and faith! This book will travel in your briefcase for years to come!

—Pastor Scott Thomas
Without Walls International Church—Central

I simply love this book. I couldn't put it down; each page inspiringly lead to the next. I love the fact that Delatorro McNeal has taken the time, done the work, compiled, and written a great book. I was empowered by his collective insight and wisdom. This book is a must-read for all those who are serious about leading a fulfilling and productive life. My heartfelt thanks goes out to Delatorro for providing us a clear way to manifest our destiny.

—George C. Fraser
Chairman and CEO, FraserNet Inc.
Author of *CLICK: Ten Truths for Building Extraordinary Relationships*

Your dream of business ownership is possible, but it takes a clear vision and deliberate, consistent steps to get there. Delatorro McNeal helps you navigate your transition one smart step at a time so you can close the gap between where you are and where you *truly* want to be.

—Valorie Burton
Best-selling author of *Why Not You? 28 Days to Authentic Confidence*

Like a friendly tour guide in a strange and foreign land, Delatorro takes us step-by-step through the process of bridging that gap between wishing and dreaming to having and doing, from mere sight-seeing to actual fusion, from looking from the outside in, to living from the inside out. He teaches us a new language, if you will, and gently leads us from existence to enjoyment, from a job to a calling, and from making money to manifesting meaning. I highly recommend this book! It will help you to release your brilliance.

—Simon T. Bailey
Professional speaker and author of *Release Your Brilliance*

I love this book. It's a true masterpiece! As an owner of five different businesses and a "pro-dreamer," I found myself unable to put down *Caught Between a Dream and a Job*. It is packed full of innovative ideas to jump-start your thinking and ignite your entrepreneurial spirit. You will find yourself empowered to stop wishing and start doing what you need to do, to get out of a dead-end job and into your lifelong dream. To those in direct sales, this is a must-read book. Don't wait until tomorrow; get it today! This book will become a bookshelf favorite for generations to come!

—Traci Bild
Author, speaker, and consultant to the direct sales industry

Can you imagine living in a world where everyone was living their dreams? Can you imagine living yours? If you've had a nagging suspicion that your life could be richer, fuller, and filled with adventure, but are unsure about how to make it happen, you're holding the book in your hands that can show you how. Quite simply, Delatorro McNeal II is my favorite kind of author: he paid attention while making his own dreams come true, and he shares what he's learned so you can too.

—Barbara J. Winters
Author of *Making a Living Without a Job*

All I can say is *wow*! I cannot wait to get copies of this book into the hands of everyone in my organization. It's an invaluable rich source of information, a must-read for everyone who wants to stop trading their time for money, own their own life, and achieve financial freedom! Delatorro's *Caught Between a Dream and a Job* is a strategic, straightforward, no-nonsense book that will empower you to take action and become who you were created to be, while you turn what you're passionate about doing into serious income!

—Karen Arena, MBA
Regional Vice President, Arbonne Independent Consultant

Amazing! You are holding in your hands the most powerful, persuasive and practical book on career transition you will ever read. It is loaded with ideas, insights, and strategies that will change your thinking and results forever. If your DREAM is bigger than your job . . . this book is for YOU.

—Jason Drenner
Speaker and author of *Little Hinges Swing Big Doors*

Delatorro McNeal gives you the inspiration, the motivation, and the clear step-by-step strategies for living the life of your dreams, on your terms. Whether you're just beginning your career path or a seasoned executive, this book is a must-read. This will be added to my "recommended reading list" that I give to my entire downline.

—Tarie MacMillian
Senior Regional Vice President, PartyLite Gifts

Caught Between a Dream and a Job represents a very good mix of self-analysis and meaningful suggestions that will ultimately influence even the most casual readers to improve their way of approaching life and career stability. This book is on its way to becoming yet another best seller for Delatorro. I highly recommend it. It is food for the soul!

—Dr. Lee Jones
President and executive editor, *InSpire* magazine

Delatorro's new book, *Caught Between a Dream and a Job*, is the road map to guide us from simply marking time in life to using time to create the life we desire and deserve. This book is a reference guide to success and should be in the library of anyone who is committed to being the best they can be.

—Tye Maner
CEO/President Tye Maner Group

Caught Between a Dream and a Job is a compilation of proven strategies, principles, and advice that if followed will aid anyone in fulfilling their God-given dreams.

—Pastor Horace E. Hockett
Born Again Church, Nashville, TN

In setting forth his own success strategies for people from all walks of life, Del is establishing himself as one of the world's great self-empowerment leaders! This book is inspiring and insightful, making the steps to reach greatness tangible and lucidly interpretable for anyone who wants to break-out of the box and reach an abundant and purposeful life!

—Damon S. Davis
Vice president and director of business development, Affiliated Media Group

Caught Between A Dream and a Job

Delatorro McNeal II

EXcel
BOOKS
A STRANG COMPANY

Most STRANG COMMUNICATIONS/CHARISMA HOUSE/SILOAM/FRONTLINE/EXCEL BOOKS/REALMS products are available at special quantity discounts for bulk purchase for sales promotions, premiums, fund-raising, and educational needs. For details, write Strang Communications/Charisma House/Siloam/FrontLine/Excel Books/Realms, 600 Rinehart Road, Lake Mary, Florida 32746, or telephone (407) 333-0600.

CAUGHT BETWEEN A DREAM AND A JOB by Delatorro L. McNeal II
Published by Excel Books
A Strang Company
600 Rinehart Road
Lake Mary, Florida 32746
www.strangdirect.com

Unless otherwise noted, all Scripture quotations are from the King James Version of the Bible.

Cover designer: Gearbox, studiogearbox.com
Executive Design Director: Bill Johnson

International Standard Book Number: 978-1-59979-333-7

First Edition

08 09 10 11 12 — 9 8 7 6 5 4 3 2 1
Printed in the United States of America

I would like to dedicate this book and its impact to several people:

- My beautiful wife, Nova McNeal, and my daughters, Miracle and Hope; you are indeed the wind beneath my wings.

- To the two people who have supported and encouraged me from the day I was born: my loving mother, Olivia B. McNeal, and my older brother, Michael T. McNeal.

- To the man who passed his greatness down to me, my loving father, Delatorro McNeal Sr.

Lastly, I would like to send out a special dedication to every dreamer, achiever, believer, survivor, overcomer, visionary, creator, innovator, pioneer, trailblazer, and entrepreneur who reads this book.

ACKNOWLEDGMENTS

THERE ARE SEVERAL PEOPLE WHO HAVE REALLY BEEN A TREMENDOUS blessing to me while I was writing this book and over the years that I have been developing the concept. So I would like to send a special thank-you to each of the following people:

Jason Drenner
Tye Maner
Jim Wilcox
Jerry Boles
Willie Jolley
Omega and Taneka Forbes
Wendi Huntley

Melonesse Wells
Matt and Shannon Bonnett
Latonya Hicks
Donna Hicks-Mitchell
Traci Bild
Joanne Wieland
Donna Cutting

Pastor Craig Altman and Grace Family Church
EmpowerMen (Ladell Cole, Tony Edwards, and Vago Lightboune)
Pastor Dwight and Jeanie Rodgers
Pastor Horace Hockett and Born Again Church
Pastor Bart Banks and St. John Progressive Church
Pastors Randy and Paula White and Without Walls Church
Pastor Scott Thomas and WWIC Central Church
Damon Davis and Affiliated Media Group

To Strang Communications and the entire editorial, marketing, PR, accounting, sales, and distribution team that takes this book all over the globe—thank you.

Additionally, I would like to thank the following people who have had a profound effect on my thinking and the success psychology that I subscribe to in this book and in life overall:

Dr. Myles Munroe
Robert Kiyosaki
Oprah Winfrey

Dr. Mike Murdock
Bishop T. D. Jakes
Anthony Robbins

Jim Rohn   Zig Ziglar

Dr. John Maxwell   Bob Proctor

Dr. Robert Anthony   Dr. Naim Akbar

Donald Trump   Michael Gerber

CONTENTS

INTRODUCTION

EMPOWERED GREETINGS, FRIEND.

Congratulations on being caught between a dream and a job. You might think that's a little weird, but I am genuinely excited for you because recognition is the first step toward real change. You can't conquer a challenge until you first identify it, and by opening this book you have identified somewhat where you are. Now let's partner together and spend the rest of this book helping you get where you really want to be.

I am so very excited that you have this book in your possession right now. I don't believe in coincidences; I believe with all my heart that there is a significant purpose, reason, and explanation as to why you and I have connected through this book. Whether you purchased this book for yourself or whether it was given to you as a gift, the impact will be the same. I believe that genuine opportunity exists in the space that lies between these words and your eyes, mind, and heart—opportunity for growth, paradigm shifts, understanding, increased wisdom, intelligent action, intentional thinking, and new beginnings.

Allow me to begin this introduction with a question:

Why are you reading this book? Please write your response in the space below.

Because I am tired of working on a 9 to 5 job. I would like to get motivated and inspired to invest in a business adventure.

It is important that you answer the previous question. Being active in this process with me will ensure that you get the most out of your experience. Whatever you wrote down as your rationale for reading this book is the same rationale for why I wrote it. Embrace the fact that I wrote this book with your

1

specific situation in mind, because I did. Right now, nobody else matters. It's just us, so let's get some real work done. You should feel special, because you are, and I take my role as not only your author but also as your coach in this process very seriously. You've made an excellence choice to read this book!

I hope that one of your reasons for reading this book is to become free! You see, the only reason you would probably be reading this book is because you feel some level of congruency between yourself and the title. Thus, you feel "caught," "stuck," and/or "trapped" in some way, and you want to be free. Free from the nine-to-five prison that robs you of your true identity and possibility. Free to live your life on your terms and become all that you were born to be. Free to take a leadership role in your own life and occupation so that you can call the shots and live your life by purposeful design rather than by mediocre default! Free to determine your own income, and free to release all of your creativity, ingenuity, and potentiality upon this world through an enterprise venture of some sort. Occupational freedom, and entrepreneurial freedom, to be more specific, is a wonderful thing, and I hope, as we take this journey together, that what's on me will rub off onto you and that you will experience life at a new level because of our time together.

Now take a moment and consider the subtitle of this book. In order to "step into the life you've always wanted," you have to be willing to step away from the life you don't want. The job you don't want. The people and paradigms that are keeping you settling for less than the best that life has to offer. You won't settle for anything less than life's best once you finish this book! So get ready, my friend! Take the twelve strategic steps with me through these life-changing chapters, and I promise you, by the time you're finished, you won't even recognize yourself anymore, because you will be a renewed individual, living life and living your dreams three-dimensionally and on purpose.

In order to get free, you have to get clarity! Clarity is power! You have to know what you want. If you are not happy with "here" and you would rather be "there," you must get absolutely clear about what "there" looks like, and this book will help you tremendously with that. This book is not about you just going out there and starting a business. Because in truth, many people who start businesses with no game plan fail miserably within the first year alone. No...no...no. This book is about discovering and uncovering the bedrock of who you really are and what you were put here to do. This book is about showing you that your DREAM is much bigger than your job! This book is about helping you to manifest the reality that you can have it all! This book is about helping you understand how to use a dream job to be your bridge from your "here" to your "there." This book is about getting you to make a choice to take a chance on yourself and the greatness that lies within you!

In order to be free, you have to get a game plan that is doable for yourself and those who are directly affected by your occupational decisions. I don't know about you, but I am tired of seeing those rags-to-riches, get-rich-tomorrow schemes that promise millions to virtually everyone, but in reality are designed to be achievable by only a select few. If you want to live your dreams at the highest level, but want a realistic game plan as to how you can do it and keep yourself and your family financially solid during the transition, then congratulations, because this book is for you!

Albert Einstein said something that I love and live by. He said, "The problems that exist in the world today cannot be solved by the level of thinking that created them."[1] Profound, profound, profound! I love this quote because it is so very true. In essence, what Einstein was trying to get us to understand is that:

1. You can't solve today's problems with yesterday's thinking.

2. You can't even solve today's problems with today's thinking.

3. The only way you can solve today's problem is to go to tomorrow's thinking!

In other words, the mind-set that got you into your current job is not the mind-set that will get you into your dream; that's yesterday's thinking. The mind-set that got you caught between your dream and your job is not the mind-set that will get you to your dream; that's today's thinking. The only mind-set that will get you to where you want to be is tomorrow's mind-set—a next-level, new paradigm mind-set; the mind-set of someone who is living the dream. That's tomorrow's thinking. Get it? Great!

The following are twelve things that I challenge and encourage you to do to maximize this experience of learning and growing together through this book.

1. Be an active reader and not a passive one. Participate with me in this book. Take notes, highlight, fold pages, fill in the blanks, and

write honest answers to the many questions I ask you throughout the book.

2. Decide right now that this book will change your life. Mark today as the first day of your new life. Literally, go to whatever calendar program or planner that you utilize most often, and write these words: *Today begins my new life.*

3. Be real with me and be real and honest with yourself. This is not the time to sugarcoat or beat around the bush. I want to help you create real change.

4. Surround yourself with positive people while experiencing, gleaning from, and transforming through this book. In fact, it may be helpful to get several people you love and cherish to get copies of this book, and you all go through it together!

5. Complete this project that you have now embarked upon. Understanding that the two hardest things to do in life are to start and finish, set your heart on finishing this book.

6. Be intentional about your success, purpose, and destiny. Remove yourself from any accidental or coincidental mind-sets.

7. Take out the trash! Yes, every now and then your old mind-set will come in direct conflict with your new developing transitional mind-set. When that happens, simply take that old stinkin' thinkin', and set it out for trash pickup.

8. Take this book one piece at a time. This is not the type of book you just whiz through so you can say you read it and check it off some list. No. This is the type of book you really want to read and chew on. Read and chew on some more. Don't rush yourself. Keep a good steady pace, do the work, take the action, and get the results.

9. Take comfort in the fact that I don't expect you to agree 100 percent with every single concept or belief I share in this book.

This book is meant to be a buffet. Take what works for you, and leave the rest on the page. However, I do challenge you to be open to new ways of looking at some things that you may have understood differently in the past.

10. Identify two or three highly positive people with whom you can share this journey of discovery and life mastery. Trust me, as you go through this book, you will be greatly enriched by having positive people from your inner circle give you feedback, confirmation, support, and encouragement.

11. Redefine and reinvent what's really possible for you.

12. Have a lot of fun learning about yourself and gaining clarity about your true wants and desires. Enjoy the journey.

Having said this, please allow me to caution you: this book will radically change your life. After experiencing this book, you will no longer be able to live an average life or have an average job. You won't be satisfied with ordinary! The extraordinary will be your new standard. You will forever be evicted from your comfort zone and placed in a mental, emotional, spiritual, social, financial, professional, and interpersonal oasis of total freedom and possibility. Applying what you learn and experience from this book will indeed have a profound affect on your life, as well as the lives of those you know and touch.

This book has been five years in the making, not because it took me five years to write it, but because of the evolution of the concept and the personal journey that I have taken with it. *Caught Between a Dream and a Job* began as a seminar that I conducted for professional associations, companies, and the general public back in 2002. The reason I created the seminar was because I figured that there had to be other people in the world out there who were just like me. At that time, I was working a nine-to-five job, but I had a dream to do something much different than what I was doing back then.

The keynote speeches and public seminars gave me enough material and coaching experience with clients and individuals to write a chapter called "Caught Between a Dream and a Job" in my second self-published book, which became a self-publishing best seller. Upon the release of that book, I was blessed to do a plethora of radio, television, and newspaper interviews based on the

Caught Between a Dream and a Job concept. It was quickly becoming a signature element for which I was known.

Now, thanks to my publishing partner Strang Communications, we have expanded this concept into a full-fledged book that has been tweaked, massaged, and tested, and now we are excited to bring it to you.

This book has seven main goals:

1. To help you to understand that you are a human being placed on this earth with a special and unique destiny. In other words, you were meant to do something very special with your life, specifically occupationally.

2. To help you to understand how your perspective toward work is directly connected to how much of your unlimited potential you will maximize. Put simply, how to live your life to the fullest through your occupation rather than settling for mediocrity.

3. To help you get crystal clear about what your life's purpose is and how to connect that purpose with your career occupation. In other words, I want to show you how to get paid to do what you love to do and were born to do.

4. To clearly define the differences between jobs and dreams, clarify their purposes, and help you uncover the plethora of lessons and experiences you have gained and will gain from both.

5. To show you how to use the power of a dream job to build a bridge from your current situation to the your ideal one.

6. To present to you the Tarzan Theory of Transition, which is the exact transition strategy that I used and have helped thousands of people utilize to make a healthy and powerful transition from their jobs to the ultimate dreams.

7. To give you immediate and executable action steps in the form of TIPS that will empower you to move from cognition to creation, and from dreaming to doing!

Ultimately, being "caught between a dream and a job" is a mind-set. So by the time you finish this book, I promise you that you will no longer be caught between a dream and a job mentally, because by the time you are done, you will have already made the move mentally, which is the most difficult part. The great news is that once you've made the mental move, the physical one is a breeze, because I am giving you a simple, step-by-step plan that anyone at any income level can follow to get the results they seek.

So my friend, the time has come to get down to the business of empowering your life and showing you how to transition from just making a living to living your making!

May only abundance and well-being abound in you,

Delatorro L. McNeal II

Section 1

Identifying Your Destiny and Purpose and the Need for a Transition

CHAPTER 1

THERE IS A PLACE CALLED "THERE"—IT'S CALLED *YOUR DESTINY*

Control your own destiny or someone else will.[1]
—Jack Welch

MANY OF US HAVE BOOKED A FLIGHT ONLINE BEFORE. WHEN YOU BEGIN to set your reservations, you have a departure city and a destination city. For example, you can't go on my travel site, www.novaltravel .com, www.orbitz.com, www.southwest.com, or any other travel site and purchase a plane ticket without knowing where you are and where you ultimately want to end up. Once you know where you are and where you want to go, the online travel booking engine works its magic to tell you which airline will take you where you want to go, at what time, and how much the trip will cost.

Basically, you start out "here," but the goal is to end up at a place called "there." "There" may be an all-inclusive resort, a fancy hotel, a mountain log cabin, a sandy beach resort with crystal blue water, a picturesque national park with all the natural beauty you can imagine, or a high-energy city with clubs, art galleries, entertainment, restaurants, bars, and attractions packed with people as far as your eyes can see. Regardless of the name you put on it, the destination is "there." It is a place of ultimate fulfillment. It has a destiny, and so do you. I believe that every human being has a destiny. We all were meant to ultimately become what we came to this earth to be. You see, the word *destination* comes from the root word *destiny*.

In this scenario, we have already learned that there are four critical components to any journey:

1. "Here," or the starting point
2. The process
3. The price
4. "There," or the end point

In order to get from here to there, we must be clear about our current location, specifically about our expected destination, be willing to go through the process, and pay the price that is required to arrive! *There is a price for everything.* For over a decade now, my motto has been "Goodness is free, but greatness will cost you. The question is, are you ready to pay the price?" "Here" has a price on it; the journey has a price; the destination has a price. Are you willing to pay the price to get unstuck? What I am talking about is moving from just job living and getting into *dream living*. Once this move happens, then you will reap the never-ending rewards of the price of that investment. We will talk more about the price in the next chapter.

Dr. Stephen Covey, whom I have had the wonderful pleasure of meeting and working with in the past, states, "We must begin with the end in mind!"[2] In other words, before we start anything, we need to have some clear idea of the end point. Think about any race you've seen on television. Whether it was a track meet, a marathon, a triathlon, or an Olympic competition, before the participants began the race, they already knew where the finish line was. They always have their destination or destiny in sight.

What about you? Do you know where your finish line is? And when I say "finish line," I am not talking about death! Yes, death is something that we all must ultimately experience; however, death and your destiny are two totally separate things. Death is the end of your life here on Earth. Destiny is the culmination and climax of your life here on Earth.

I believe it was the great twenty-first-century philosophers Bart and Lisa Simpson who made the following statement famous: "Are we there yet? Are we there yet? Are we there yet?" They, like all of us, were anxious to get to the "there" in their own lives. What about us? What about society? What about you? Are you excited about your "there"? Do you fully realize that you were deposited on this earth with a "there"—a "there" that both you and God created before you were born? What do you see when you envision your "there"? I may have never met you before, but allow me to tell you what I see when I envision your "there":

- I see a place where you get up each morning excited about the day.

- I see a place where it's sometimes hard to sleep at night because of all the wonderful ideas that you think up and are eager to implement.

- I see a place where there is no lid or cap on how much money you can earn.

- I see a place where you are celebrated and your gifts are maximized.

- I see a place where you are loved and appreciated for the difference you make.

- I see a place where your family and close friends speak well of you daily.

- I see a place where your gifts flow in such a fashion that time stands still.

- I see a place where you call the shots and take ownership of your future.

- I see a place where you take vacations and minivacations as often as you like because you determine your own schedule.

- I see a place where you live your life by design and not by default.

- I see a place where every failure in your life—because you learn from it—automatically turns into a life lesson that you use to empower yourself and others.

- I see a place where you can give back to others and mentor, coach, and develop others to do what you do so well.

- I see a place where you can look up and know that God is pleased with the imprint that you are making upon this world—one day and one life at a time.

- I see a place where you attract into your life all that you desire for yourself.

- I see a place where you are at the top and are pulling others up to the top with you.

Now it's your turn. Tell me what you see when you envision your "there." When you consider the subtitle of this book in terms of stepping into the life you've always wanted, what do you see?

_____

_____

_____

Doesn't that place look, sound, smell, taste, and feel great? Well, let's get there!

It has been said that success is not about the destination; it's about the journey. As a professional speaker, I used to agree with and promote this statement from the stage. But I no longer agree with this adage, because in truth, I believe that success is about both—the journey (the process) and the destination (the end result or final outcome). In other words, it's about the process toward and the achievement of the end goal. If success was just about the journey, then people all over the world would enjoy riding around in a car and never getting out of the car because the final destination—the mall, work, the park, the gym, or a relative's house—would not matter. Pilots would take off from one city, fly all the way to the next city, and turn back around midair and land back in the departure city because success would be just about the journey, not the arrival. So you see, success, which (according to Webster's dictionary) is defined simply as a "favorable or desired outcome," can't just be found in the journey. Although enjoying the journey is important, we all still want to get there! We want to arrive at our ultimate destination.

> You will know you have arrived at your "there" when people can see you from a distance flowing in your gifts and talents and can't determine with congruent exactitude whether you are working hard or playing hard.

Think about it. When you awake each morning and head to work, you get into your car, onto a plane, into a cab, onto a public transportation system, or begin walking or biking with the ultimate goal of what? *Arriving!* You want to get *there*, and you have full expectation of it! In the process of getting there, you make the most of your journey. That may include listening to music and/or talk radio, reading the morning paper or a magazine, enjoying inspirational materials (audiobooks, CDs, DVDs), talking on the phone, putting on makeup, shaving, eating, having dialogue with other passengers, or even sleeping as long as you are not the one in control of the steering wheel. So we enjoy the journey and fill our time during the journey with things that prepare us for the destination, but again, we have full expectation of getting there.

My friend, there is a "there" in your life, an ever-evolving, always-expanding, always-encouraging place where you were meant to arrive and dwell. Some people believe and teach that your destiny is 100 percent predetermined and that destiny, fate, and/or the hand of God have 100 percent control over your life to place you into your destiny regardless of your action or inaction. I beg to differ!

While I do believe your destiny, your ultimate place of fulfillment—*there*— was divinely selected and entrusted to you by God, it is still up to you to arrive at it. In other words, you were meant to do something and be someone of greatness; however, your thoughts, your decisions, your actions, and your associations are what will guarantee or hinder your arrival. God gifted each of us with free will. So if it is your will to be free—free from the nine-to-five grind of just working to pay bills—then this is the book you have been longing for! Congratulations, you have attracted this solution into your life.

Now, imagine going to a restaurant and being seated. You review the menu as the waiter or waitress explains the day's special. Then you place your order, all the while having an enjoyable dialogue with your lunch companions. Sounds pretty normal, right? Now imagine that the food that you have ordered, waited for, and are now salivating over never arrives at your table. I mean, it just never comes. How crazy, frustrating, annoying, disappointing, and ultimately dissatisfying would that be? Would you ever want to eat at that restaurant again? Probably not.

As crazy as it would be to eat at a restaurant that allows you to enjoy the process of ordering and waiting but not the delivery and consumption of your meal, it is equally as crazy to live a life where you go through the process of day-to-day living without ever fulfilling your destiny. What's worse is to sentence yourself to an existence where you don't enjoy the day-to-day journey *and* you don't arrive at the final destination. What a tragedy! In that scenario you existed, but you never lived! That is why I wrote this book. You are why I wrote this book. I wanted to sound the alarm and wake you up to the reality that you are an amazing human spirit placed here on Earth with a special purpose and destiny that should enable you to impact the lives of others and be compensated simultaneously.

TRUE SUCCESS DEFINED

I believe that it is critical to define success for yourself. You must come up with a working definition as to what success means to you. The reality is that everyone wants to be successful, but few have taken the time to qualify and quantify what success is so that they can realistically attain it. Instead, choosing to be followers rather than leaders, people succumb to whatever definition society gives to success. Don't measure your life with someone else's measuring stick. Define success for yourself. To some people, success is millions, if not billions, of dollars in the bank. To others, success is being a good citizen and living a healthy life. Yet to others, success is starting and growing a successful business, writing a best-selling book, developing commercial real estate, raising great kids, or winning a presidential election. None of these are any greater or less than the other; they are just different. So with that in mind, feel free to define your idea of success, and be clear about it. How can you hit a target that you cannot see, and furthermore, how can you hit a target that you don't have? Before we go any further, let's stop now and define your idea of success.

How do you define *success*? Go ahead. Tell me. What does *success* mean to you?

_____

_____

_____

I believe that true success is doing what you love to do, doing the thing that you were born to do, and being paid well to do it. Period! I believe that this is real success. The unfortunate reality, though, is that most people never adopt this as their right, responsibility, or goal. Therefore, few really achieve it. Most people end up working a job, doing what they don't like for the majority of their lives, for the primary purpose of paying bills, and they end up, as is often said, "meandering in the maze of mediocrity." But I am excited because you will be different, your life will be different, and your story will end differently because you are reading and actively applying this book to your life.

THE MASTER IN THE ART OF LIVING

I would like to share a quotation with you that I have been sharing with my audiences and coaching clients for many years now. You may have heard of it before, but if not, I am thrilled to introduce it to you. It is by James A. Michener.

> The master in the art of living makes little distinction between,
> His work and his play,
> His labor and his leisure,
> His mind and his body,
> His information and his recreation,
> His love and his religion.
> He hardly knows which is which.
> He simply pursues his vision of excellence in whatever he does,
> Leaving others to decide whether he is working or playing.
> To him, he's always doing both.[3]

Take a moment to read the quote again. Now tell me, what does it mean to you?

_____

_____

_____

This quotation is so profound to me because it is the essence of what this entire book and concept is all about. "OK, Delatorro," you may be saying to me, "I get the fact that there is a 'there' for me, but how will I know when I have arrived? And how does this quote apply to my destiny?" Excellent questions. You will know when you have arrived at your "there" when your life is in harmony with this quotation. You will know when people can see you from a distance flowing in your gifts and talents and can't determine with congruent exactitude whether you are working hard or playing hard. When your life's work becomes what you do for work, then you have arrived at the place called "there." But remember, even once you get there, there are many different levels of "there" to aspire to and attain, which means we never stop growing and giving. We just keep climbing to higher heights and taking as many people along with us as we can.

My friend, there is a difference between existing efficiently (which is what most people do) and living abundantly (which is what few people tend to do). You see, most people are just going along to get along. They are just trying to survive life, struggling to make the most of their lives, while spending the majority of their creative energy watching other people live the lives they wished they were living. That's garbage! You are far too special and unique for that. We need you! Yes, *we* need *you* to operate at the fullness of your purpose and destiny so that *we* can benefit from *your greatness*. Life mastery begins with destiny and purpose discovery. I am excited to be with you on what will prove to be a very powerful and life-altering ride.

MANY NAMES FOR THE SAME THING

Much of what we are talking about so far should not sound completely foreign to you. You have probably heard some of this information before. It probably sounds a lot like common sense, right?

Everything God created has a natural flow, and when it operates in that flow, there is little struggle.

However, please remember that common sense is not common practice. Just because we know better does not always mean that we do better. That's exactly why knowledge alone is *not* power! Applied knowledge is what creates power. You see, information without application will lead to frustration. But information with application gets you powerfully to your destination!

Confirmation and agreement are two wonderful gifts that I believe God and life give us to keep us on track in a particular direction we are going or on the course of right action we are taking. Well, this place that we are talking about in this chapter, your "there" or your destiny, has been given many different names, and experts over the years have taught the principle using various terminologies. Here are a few examples:

- Dr. Myles Munroe calls it maximizing your life's purpose and potential.

- Dr. Mike Murdock calls it fulfilling your life's assignment.

- Max Lucado calls it living in your sweet spot.

- Metaphysicians call it living in your flow state.

- Joseph Campbell calls it following your bliss.

- Spiritual experts call it living in your zone.

- Anthony Robbins calls it mastering your destiny.

- Pastors and evangelists refer to it as answering your call.

- Donald Trump calls it living your passion.

- In the movie *Jerry Maguire*, Cuba Gooding Jr.'s character calls it achieving the quan.

As you can see, this concept is widely accepted and supported by many in the field of human, personal, spiritual, professional, and financial development. Take this as confirmation that you are headed in the right direction. Now, hopefully you will accept this concept. Don't get tripped up on the labels that people put on it. It's the same thing. The important thing is not that you know all the terms but that you know how to apply this knowledge to your life to get the results you want.

STRONG STATEMENTS

Let me be frank! We all know the numbers. The average human being spends a little over one-third of his/her life working. That breaks down to 2,080 hours a year. When multiplied by forty years, which is the average career span of people working jobs until retirement, we get a total of 83,200 hours in the lifespan of the average human being working a job.

The average employee spends ten hours per day at work, eight hours per day sleeping, and six hours per day at "home," which could include any of the following activities: going to the gym or grocery store, cooking and eating dinner, being involved in a child's extracurricular activities, watching TV, surfing the Internet, attending midweek personal/spiritual growth events, and spending time with family.

What's the point? You spend too much of your lifetime working to do what you hate! You spend too much of your daily life working to hate what you do!

You were designed, wired, and built for better than what you've settled for!

When you do what you were created and born to do, there is a flow in your life. Go with that flow, not against it. It's there for a reason. Think about it. Everything God created has a natural flow, and when it operates in that flow, there is little struggle.

- Grass does not struggle to grow.
- Water does not struggle to flow.
- Wind does not struggle to blow.
- Clouds do not struggle to float.
- Rain does not struggle to fall.
- The sun does not struggle to shine.
- The earth does not struggle to rotate on its axis.
- Birds do not struggle to chirp.
- Dogs do not struggle to bark.
- Flowers do not struggle to bloom.

Human beings are God's greatest creation because we, out of all of these creations, were the only creatures made specifically in His image and likeness. So why do we struggle so much? Better yet, why do we sentence ourselves to a life of struggling to make it through work every week? Why do we allow ourselves to live lives of quiet desperation, wishing that we lived in a state of flow that we were born with? It does not make sense, and again, that's why I wrote this book.

I am convinced that when we become a nation and a world full of people who do what they were born to do, and flow exclusively in that, we will have much better, cleaner, healthier neighborhoods and communities; stronger and more connected families; and thriving marriages and relationships. However, as long as most people continue to trade their time for a paycheck that they have already outgrown, in a job that they dislike and that dwarfs their potential and imprisons their purpose, we will continue to see a decline in the nucleus and fabric of our society. The conditioning of society has contributed greatly to the way that we live and the problem that we face of most people being caught between a dream and a job. Here are a few examples of what I am talking about.

- We live in a society that educates us to work for someone else the rest of our lives.

- We live in a society that promotes money over meaning.

- We live in a society that pushes us to pursue a paycheck and not our purpose.

- We live in a society that tells us to chase dollars, not our destiny.

- We live in a society that values the bling-bling more than the main thing.

- We live in a society that teaches us to compete rather than to complete.

Yes, money is important and critical for us to live and provide for our families. But the problem is that we think, or we have been conditioned to believe, that we must cash in personal fulfillment for financial security, and that is not true. Money is important, but guess what? You can have it all. You can have meaning and make money.

Dr. John Maxwell, whom I consider to be one of my mentors, told me something powerful over lunch one day. He said, "Delatorro, if you commit yourself to making a difference, making a dollar is not hard!" I love that.

So now that we know what society thinks and how it feels, let's scrap all of that and pursue a new paradigm. Don't follow society's standards or you will be sentenced to a life of average. Nobody

> Life is supposed to look better in front of you rather than behind you.

wants that. We all want the best and the most of what life has to offer. After all, we only get one shot at this gift called life. This life is neither a practice nor a dress rehearsal; it is the real deal.

"YOUOLOGY" 101

You were put here with a "there"! You know it. I can tell you know it, because you are still reading. If this book, this content, this message did not resonate with you, you would have stopped reading by now.

You were wired, engineered, created, manufactured, produced, assembled, constructed, and developed with a there—an ultimate place where you are supposed to live and thrive. In addition to that, you were blessed with all the tools (talents, gifts, abilities, personality traits, temperaments, ambitions, and passions) necessary to get you to your destiny and sustain you in your destiny. All those tools are inside you right now. Right now!

You have been deposited into this world because of your wanting to be here and because of God's desire and magnificent creation of this masterpiece that we call you.

You were born loaded, rich, wealthy, and abundant! That was your original and initial state of being. The funny thing is that on the surface, we think these terms apply only to money. But in truth, when you consider that the average human has over six hundred undiscovered talents, according to Rick Warren's best seller *The Purpose-Driven Life*,[4] then you realize that we really are rich in resources, talents, skills, abilities, and ideas that we have to pull from to live our purpose and fulfill our destiny. You have everything you need; it's just a matter of you recognizing it. We will talk more about this later in the book.

You, yes, you—not just the rich people, the famous people, the folks you see on TV, the folks you read about in the news, the folks that have their own Web sites, or whatever—have a destiny, and a large part of that destiny is for you to leave this world better than the way you found it.

A good speaker friend of mine is a gentleman by the name of Mark Scharenbroich. He has won the highest awards in existence for professional speakers through the National Speakers Association (NSA). I was in the audience when he spoke at the 2005 NSA National Convention. He shared something that absolutely changed my paradigm about destiny. At the conclusion of his speech, he mentioned three pieces of advice he would share with anyone coming behind him in life. He said:

1. Know what matters.
2. Enjoy the journey.
3. Leave the campsite better than the way you found it.

Number three is what messed me up! Mark said that life is supposed to look better behind you than it does in front of you. This was a major paradigm shift for me because for many years, I told people that life is supposed to look better in front of you rather than behind you. And when it comes to vision, it should. The rest of your life should be the best of your life. However, when it comes to impact, the world should look better behind you than in front of you because the world behind you has your footprint on it. It should look better because you have lived. Not existed, but lived. Not jobbed, but dreamed! Not settled, but seized all that life had to offer!

In conclusion, just take a moment and imagine our world without the impact, influence, imagination, genius, contribution, and footprint of people who achieved their destiny. Do you remember earlier when I told you that we need you? What I mean by that is that you have a gift inside you that only you possess; however, it was meant to benefit this world in some way. So when you use that gift to it's fullest potential and contribute to society and the world, you end up making the kind of imprint on the world like these people made: Mahatma Gandhi, Martin Luther King Jr., Mother Teresa, George Washington Carver, Joel Osteen, Thurgood Marshall, Oprah Winfrey, Barack Obama, James Brown, Walt Disney, Zig Ziglar, Babe Ruth, Michael Jordan, John F. Kennedy, Colin Powell, Bill Gates, Warren Buffet, T. D. Jakes, Billy Graham, Prince, Madonna, Celine Dion, David Yonggi Cho, Winston Chuchill, Albert Einstein, Sir Oliver Wendell Holmes, John Maxwell, Malcolm X, Harriett Tubman, and millions more.

Since these people are what we would probably call famous or world renowned, let's bring it down to not just the world but more specifically to your world. Give me the names of some of the people who, because they achieved their destiny, have positively impacted your life in a special way. They could be relatives, friends, business colleagues, mentors, college friends, world leaders, or just people you admire.

_____

_____

_____

Now, let me ask you one final question. Do you think that these people would want you settling for a job or thriving in your dream? I think we both know the answer to that!

CHAPTER SUMMARY

EIGHT POINTS TO PONDER
DURING YOUR TRANSITION

1. You were created before you were born, and you were born with a "there"! You were engineered with a propensity toward your destiny!

2. There are four components to any journey to your destiny: (1) "here," or the starting point, (2) the process, (3) the price, and (4) "there," or the end point.

3. Success is about both enjoying the journey and arriving at the destination.

4. True success is doing what you love to do—the things that you were born to do—and being paid well to do them.

5. You spend too much of your life working to hate or dislike what you do!

6. When your life's work becomes what you do for work, then you've arrived at your destiny. You were not meant to struggle all your life. You're supposed to flow!

7. You can have it all. You can have money and live a life of meaning. You can make a difference and make a dollar at the same time!

8. You were put here to leave this world better than the way you found it.

CHAPTER 2

WHOEVER TOLD YOU TO JOB?

What work I have done I have done because it has been play.
If it had been work I shouldn't have done it. Who was it who
said, "Blessed is the man who has found his work"? Whoever
it was had the right idea in his mind. Mark you, he says his
work—not somebody else's work. The work that is really a
man's own work is play and not work at all. Cursed is the
man who has found some other man's work and cannot lose
it. When we talk about the great workers of the world, we
really mean the great players of the world.[1]

—Mark Twain

work \ wurk \ *n* 1 : activity in which one exerts
strength or faculties to do or perform something 2 : sustained physical or mental effort
to overcome obstacles and achieve an objective
or result 3 : the labor, task, or duty that
is one's accustomed means of livelihood 4 : a
specific task, duty, function, or assignment
often being a part or phase of some larger
activity.

E VERY DAY, BILLIONS OF PEOPLE ALL OVER THE GLOBE WAKE UP EACH morning and go to work. They utilize their gifts, talents, abilities, skills, trades, vocations, ideas, mind-sets, bodies, and brains to exert effort in a specific function with the goal of producing a result and, ultimately, a paycheck.

In our society and in our world we identify ourselves highly with our work. Our work is one of our most predominate ways that we classify and categorize ourselves. Think about it; when you first meet someone you've never met, you ask him or her their name. What do you typically ask them next? You ask them what they do for a living. If the person is a student, you ask them what school they attend and, immediately following that, what course of study they are majoring in or focusing on, which gives you insight as to what they want to do for a living. If you meet someone who is retired, after learning about how they are enjoying retirement, you immediately want to know what work they retired from. When you are with a friend, business colleague, or family member and you see someone you know off in the distance, you typically lean over to the person you are with and say, for example, "Oh, look, that's Christine! She's an attorney." Thus, outside of our names, and sometimes birthplaces, the next most common identifying characteristic about a person is their work.

> Be the change that you want to see in the world![2]
>
> —Mahatma Gandhi

Work is our livelihood; it's the thing we do to provide for our loved ones and ourselves. And it is supposed to be the thing that we do to leave our footprint of positive difference upon this world.

Work is such a vital part of our day-to-day lives that most people wrap their entire lives around their work. How can you tell? Well, just think about it. You probably plan the majority of the important things in your day and in your life around your work. For example:

- Most vacations are planned around when people can get time off from work.

- Most weddings and honeymoons are planned around getting time off from work.

- Most people plan their families and birthing of children around how much time they will be able to take off from work.

- Most people's mealtime, free time, and "me" time are all framed around work.

- Most after-school programs are designed to give children something to do and a place to go until their parents get off of work.

- Most people's extracurricular activities are done either early in the morning or in the late afternoon because that's before or after what? Work!

EXISTING VERSUS LIVING

Because of the enormous role that work plays in our daily lives (we learned in chapter 1 that the average person will spend 83,200 hours in their lifetime working), how we approach work and how we live our lives while we work is a vital part of how content we become and how full of a life we live. I believe that you really have not lived until you have found your life's work and worked it to the maximum. Life presents us with two choices. We can either exist efficiently or live abundantly.

Both choices have a price tag on them. The price for existing efficiently is that you tend to lead a very shallow, empty, and frustrated life, far below your potential and your privilege. The cost of living abundantly is that you must get out all that lies within you and become the person that you have always wanted to be, not only for yourself but also for the benefit of others in this world. The moment you realize and internalize that your becoming better makes the world better, your life changes. We've been lied to! We think that in order to create world change we have to hold some large political office, be some wealthy business tycoon, or be some famous, celebrated world figure. But nothing could be further from the truth. Want some truth? The truth is that you, yes, you, can change this world for the better just by the way you approach your work and life.

> What a tragedy to have existed and never lived!
> —Dr. Myles Munroe

Just by deciding that you will live abundantly changes the world. Imagine our world if people stopped existing and really started living. Crime would almost disappear because when people live, they don't need to take from or harm others to get what they want, because they realize that what they really want, they already have within them. It's just a matter of recognition and development. Thus, people would invest their time in developing themselves rather than tearing down others.

However, as long as people are just "existing" and struggling through life, day in and day out, we will always have people who feel that the best way to get ahead is to push others down or behind them, and that is simply ineffective. Crime is proof of the fact that we have not learned to value ourselves and others.

I would venture to say that 90 percent of our current workforce, whether they enjoy what they do or not, are existing efficiently rather than living abundantly. I can tell because everywhere I go, I see people fast-forwarding their lives. On Monday mornings, the first thing you hear most people say is, "Oh, I just can't wait till it's Friday!" People live their lives with the fast-forward button on. They come into work Monday, and just like in the movie *Click* with Adam Sandler, they try to fast-forward past the day-to-day reality just to get to the weekend again. If you have ever done this, said this, or repeatedly felt this way, then up until now you have been existing efficiently. You've been getting by, making it, fairing well, or just coasting through life. Not anymore. Up until now, you've done an efficient job of existing, but from now on, you are going to start being effective at living, loving, and learning your life. Congratulations! From now on, no more fast-forwarding, and no more rewinding; we are going to allow our lives to powerfully play out in our favor! Deal or no deal?

FRAMING YOUR LIFE

Live life three-dimensionally! You see, most people live life one-dimensionally. They live the length of their years and celebrate birthdays, which is good, however, if you live and die only celebrating birthdays, then you lived one-dimensionally. Life was meant to be lived three-dimensionally. You are supposed to live the length, width, and depth of your years. So live, learn, and love long, wide, and deep! That's real living![3]

—Nido Qubein

Most people—the 90 percent who exist rather than live and those who live one-dimensionally rather than three-dimensionally—frame their lives around their work. In reality it should be the exact opposite. You should frame your work around your life! People who live (and I mean really live) life to the fullest frame their work around their lives. As long as you are forcing your life to be molded, shaped, framed, formed, and fashioned after your work (even worse, a job that you don't enjoy), you will always put too much pressure on the work to satisfy you in life, and it never will.

Current job satisfaction statistics tell us that:
» 72 percent of executives declare that they are not in their dream jobs.[4]
» 87 percent of Americans dislike their jobs.[5]
» Less than 50 percent of Americans feel satisfied with their jobs.[6]
» 33 percent of Americans hate their jobs.[7]
» 25 percent of employees view their jobs as their number-one stressor in life.[8]
» 41 percent of Americans admit that they live paycheck to paycheck.[9]
» 70 percent of people are not motivated or competent to perform the basics of their jobs.[10]
» 70 percent of people work without much enthusiasm or passion.[11]
» 43 percent of employees feel angry toward their employers because of being overworked.[12]
» 50 percent of employees believe that they are underpaid.[13]
» 70 percent of hourly, nonunion employees are likely to look for new jobs.[14]
» Over 60 percent of employees are looking for new jobs in the next three months.[15]
» 66 percent of tenured employees plan to find new jobs within the next three months.[16]
» HR experts estimate the hard costs to replace an employee to be at 33 percent and 50 percent of the base salary of that employee, and this does not include soft costs such as loss of productivity, institutional knowledge, and new hire recruiting and training expenses.[17]
» 67 percent of Americans labor in the wrong career field.[18]

Statistics like these bring home the reality that you and I were never meant to permanently stay in a job situation. You were put here for more than that. Your purpose is too big for any singular job title, and this information just further proves that fact. And what's worse is that when there's low job satisfaction, there is also low life satisfaction. Because so much of our life is spent at work, it's hard to have one without the other. This whole notion of job satisfaction is such a moving target because of two things. First, there are at least fourteen different factors that play into job satisfaction, making it difficult to align them all in the favor of employees with varying tastes. Below are just some of the factors that play into job satisfaction.

> My priorities have always been God first, family second, career third. I have found that when I put my life in this order, everything seems to work out.
>
> —Mary Kay Ash

- Salary
- Benefits
- Cleanliness and safety
- Technology and resources
- Job training and development
- Communication channels
- Workload
- Promotion policies and bonuses
- Vacation and sick leave
- Cultural and gender diversity
- Leadership and mentoring
- Reward and recognition programs
- Commute
- Quality friendships

Second, the word *satisfaction* is a moving target because what satisfies someone today may not satisfy them tomorrow. People are picky. From an employer standpoint, I can see how it is difficult to try to keep everyone happy. The older generations are easier to satisfy, according to a study by TNS for the Conference Board, but with generations X and Y in the workforce now, things have become much harder. See these statistics:

- Less than two out of every five workers under the age of twenty-five are satisfied with their jobs. This segment of the population has the lowest level of satisfaction currently and the lowest level ever recorded in the nearly twenty-year history of this survey.

- Workers ages forty-five to fifty-four expressed the second lowest level of satisfaction with less than 45 percent content with their current job.

- At the other end of the scale are workers ages fifty-five to sixty-four and sixty-five and over. Nearly half of all workers in these age groups are satisfied with their employment situation.[19]

Do you see now why it's dangerous to frame your life around your work? Who would want to frame their lives around those statistics? Not me. If your work comes first, then everything else in your life takes a backseat to your work—your social life, spiritual life, personal life, family life, and so on. That means that your life is forced to react to your work. And if your work is not enjoyable or is not a source of pleasure to you, everything else suffers or you must work twice as hard to counterbalance your work. This becomes a domino effect, which means when something goes wrong at work, since you've framed your life around it, then automatically and almost by default, something will go wrong in your personal life or at home! It's a snowball effect that most people live with every day, and many become numb and desensitized to after a while. This is not an effective or efficient way to live.

> I believe that you are your work. Don't trade the stuff of your life, or your time, for nothing more than dollars. That's a rotten bargain.
>
> —Rita Mae Brown

Think about it like this: Let's say I asked you to make a sculpture out of a Coke bottle and some clay. Now imagine your work as the Coke bottle and your life as clay. In the current scenario, you would basically attach the clay to the bottle the best way you can and pack it on really good. But no matter how colorful, how textured, or how attractive the clay is, the final sculpture will probably look like the Coke bottle. The clay was forced to take the shape of what came before it in priority, which was work.

Now let's use the exact same materials, but now the Coke bottle represents your life—your joys, your talents, and your skills and abilities that you do with ease and enjoyment. Now let's say that the clay represents work or how you make your living. No matter how you form and fashion that clay (work), the final sculpture is still drastically impacted by what came first—your quality life! And that's how it should be. You should be wrapping your work around your life and not wrapping your life around your job! If you are forming your life around your work, then you are "jobbing," not working. Whoever told you to job?

If you are feeling like I am all in your business at this point in the book, that is a very good thing. But don't feel bad. Feel empowered, because I promise you, I will give you answers to the questions that your mind and heart are asking. Additionally, understand this; you are not alone. I believe that most people allow work to frame their lives—so much so that most people give their best to their work and their leftovers to their life! Think about it; most people look their best physically (hair, nails, wardrobe, makeup, breath, and so on) at work. They even give their best attitude, disposition, and personality to the job, and then they go home and transform into their real selves for those that they love most. And who suffers? The significant other, the spouse, the children, the friends, and the family—those whom we really care about the most. What a tragedy!

> Never continue in a job you don't enjoy. If you're happy in what you're doing, you'll like yourself; you'll have inner peace. And if you have that, along with physical health, you will have had more success than you could possibly have imagined.[20]

Married couples know this better than anyone. We've all experienced the times when the spouse looks like "plain Jane" or "plain Jim" around the house until it's time to go to work. Then, all of sudden, the metamorphosis takes place. In our personal lives we can be late for dinner with friends, late to a movie, late to a school play, late to church, even late to a ball game for our kids and think nothing of it. But Monday through Friday we will almost run over a turtle in the middle of the road to get to work on time! We take our professional lives much more seriously then we do our personal lives. Affairs at work are so common and easy to initiate because when we are at work, we put on our best and try to put our best foot forward, which is what we should do. However, in truth, we should try to give our best to everyone, especially to those we love. At work we are only seeing the mask that a person wears each day to fulfill an occupational requirement. They are playing a role, and we are seeing a portion of them, not the real person, and certainly not the total package. If we really knew the rest of them, we probably would not be as impressed. So we have to draw the line and stop cashing in personal contentment for professional gain, especially when in reality we can have them both. Yes, you can have them both. But in order to get them, you have to work your dream, not just work a job. Again, I ask you, whoever told you to job?

Society conditions us to make first priority the thing that makes money, not that which gives us meaning! There is a scene in the movie *The Devil Wears Prada* where Andy, a new intern at a fashion magazine, is finally making some headway in her new job. She says to her mentor Nigel, "It's a busy day. . . . My personal life is hanging on by a thread." Nigel, who is equally swamped at work and dying for a personal life, says back to her, "Join the club. That's what happens when you start doing well at work. Let me know when your whole life goes up in smoke. That means it's time for a promotion!"

Again, this is the mind-set that we have adopted in our society. And in that movie, just like in real life, it took Andy almost losing everything she really loved and enjoyed for her to realize that she could have it all, but she had to be willing to pay the price of letting go of the wrong thing to embrace the right thing!

> Doing what you like is freedom. Liking what you do is happiness.
> —Johnny Carson

Success is an inside-out process. Allow me to illustrate what I mean by that. Take the word *profession*, and within that word you will find the letters that spell the word *person*.

- PRofEsSiON yields PERSON

- PRofEsSiONAL yields PERSONAL

There is a person within every profession, and personal fulfillment creates professional fulfillment. Professional growth can't take place without personal growth. Once we understand the true order that our life is supposed to be in, and once we understand that success is an inside to outside transmogrifica-tion, we then work harder on improving ourselves at the personal level so that improvement at the professional level becomes an automatic by-product.

Now, going back to the Coke bottle illustration, let's try framing our work around our life! This means that the things you enjoy most about yourself and your life come first, and then you form, frame, shape, and configure a livelihood around that! In this instance, you are forcing work to adjust to the best parts of you—the parts of you that you enjoy. Your personal passions, gifts, and talents now take front seat and dictate your work or, better yet, become your work.

That's powerful! Again, that is doing what you love, enjoy, and are willing to master, and having people pay you to do it.

Part of the problem has been that we live in a society that does not teach this. Most of our society teaches people to get a good education and then get a job! In our country, the educational system is still in large part framed around the industrial age and has not fully adapted itself to the present information age and the coming age of the entrepreneur as Michael Gerber speaks of. However there is hope. According to research done by the Ewing Marion Kauffman Foundation, the numbers of U.S. colleges and universities that now offer courses on entrepreneurship have drastically increased. Out of the 4,000 colleges and universities that exist in the U.S. today, in 1985 there where only 300 institutions that taught courses on entrepreneurship. In 1991, the number rose to 1,000 institutions, and in 2005 there were 1,992 institutions of the 4,000 teaching courses on entrepreneurship. So a necessary shift is beginning to take place.[21]

> Not long ago, the world belonged to individuals whose thinking was characterized by objectivity and analysis.... "The future belongs to creators and empathizers, pattern recognizers and meaning-makers. We are moving from an economy built on logical, linear capabilities to one built on the inventive, empathic capabilities of what's rising in it's place: the Creative Age."[22]

THE EVOLUTION OF THE WORK AGES

It is important that we understand the age in which we are now working so that we can best adapt to it, maximize it, and eventually take a leadership role within it. But first, let's go back in history briefly to understand where we have come from. The first stage of mankind's evolution in the workforce was hunting and gathering, which took the most basic of skills and understanding. We took great strides when our distant ancestors recognized the gift of the agricultural age through the multiplicity of seedtime and harvest. Small gardens that used to feed families quickly became major crops that would assist in feeding the nation. Both small and large corporations incorporated the gift of multiplicity into our nation during the industrial age. The Industrial Revolution caused a major shift of technological, socioeconomic, and cultural conditions in the mid-eighteenth century and early nineteenth century. It began in Britain and spread throughout the world. During that time, an economy based on manual labor was replaced by one dominated by industrial and mechanical manufacturing.

The gift of multiplicity was best seen through assembly lines for mass production. Additionally, during this time Henry Ford became a business tycoon with his invention of the Model T, our first mass-produced automobile. After the Industrial Revolution, our society gave way to the global information age. The information age is a name given to the period after the industrial age and before the knowledge economy.[23] *Information age* is a term applied to the period where information rapidly propagated, more narrowly applying to the 1980s onward. Some have argued that the pinnacle of the information age was in or around the time of 1989, during the fall of the Berlin wall. Under conventional economic theory, the information age also heralded the era where information was a scarce resource, and its capture and distribution generated competitive advantage. Bill Gates, the wealthiest man in the world, according to *Forbes* magazine, created Microsoft, and it became one of the largest companies in the world based on its influence in creating the underlying mechanics to facilitate global information distribution. One could argue, though, that it actually began during the latter half of the nineteenth century with the invention of the telephone and telegraph. It is often used in conjunction with the term *postindustrial society.*

When information became more accessible, the knowledge economy commenced. The knowledge economy started around 1992 and continued to approximately 2002. The current economic era is defined as the intangible economy. Both the knowledge economy and intangible economy have set the stage for what some great minds have called the creative age, which we are now in.[24]

Simply put, this is the age of the dreamer, the visionary, the entrepreneur, and people of passion. This is the age that the late greats like James Allen, Wallace Wattles, Napoleon Hill, and Earl Nightingale have all spoken of. This is the age that, "Whatever the mind of man can conceive and believe, it can achieve."[25] What a great age to be alive! All of the ages that came before merely set the stage for you to stand up and show off the dreams and passions within you. Think about it—with the introduction of each age, there has been a drastic change in the way we work. And now with the information age and creative age here, we have the benefit of all the ages that come before. We have the ability to grow our own food and mass-produce products and services. We have global communication through the Internet, and technology is ever expanding and is now affordable to almost anyone. So indeed, the stage is set for people to begin to really create, innovate, and dominate. At the dawning of each new age, entrepreneurs, innovators, and inventors took on the challenge and changed the face of work as we knew it. The old advice to go to school and get a good education so you can get a good, safe, secure job is outdated indeed.

> **Work joyfully and peacefully, knowing that right thoughts and right efforts will inevitably bring about right results.**[26]
>
> —James Allen

We now know that we are in the information age and creative age, where job loyalty has become a thing of the past, on the side of both the employer and the employee. Companies today have to compete on a global scale, and consumers are smarter now then ever before. So companies can't just get by on a good name; they now have to compete on product quality, price, and service at the international level. Thus companies are no longer loyal to people working jobs but rather to processes that will allow them to streamline and maximize profits. On the flip side, in today's bling-bling, consumer-driven society where the focus is so much on material things, people are no longer loyal to companies that pay less. Today, people will quit a job simply for one dollar more per hour somewhere else.

YOU ARE SUPPOSED TO WORK, NOT JOB!

From the beginning of time, work has been a cornerstone component of our life experience on this earth. Work is critical, practical, social, political, financial, biblical, psychological, emotional, familial, physical, spiritual, and tangible. Work is a vital part of our world. Imagine for a second what it would be like if for one day—just one day—nobody worked. There would be utter chaos everywhere. Because the reality is that, as I told you in chapter 1, we all need each other. We all need each person to show up and work our individual and unique purpose.

I believe that your work was never meant to be just a job. I believe that everyone and everything was meant to work or function according to its purpose. Look at the list below:

- Cars work.
- Cell phones work.
- CDs work.
- Microwaves work.
- Gaming systems work.
- Dishwashers work.
- Refrigerators work.
- Candles work.
- Chairs work.
- Watches work.
- Planes work.
- Subway systems work.
- Money works.
- Buses work.
- Computers work.
- DVDs work.
- TVs work.
- Remotes work.
- Windows work.
- Washers and dryers work.
- Light switches work.
- Clocks work.
- Traffic lights work.
- Trains work.
- The Internet works.
- People work.

Although people are not objects or machines, there is a natural flow that appears in the list above. All these things were created for a purpose, and they work effectively and effortlessly within that purpose. Notice that all of these things work; they don't job, going from one meaningless task to another! All that they do plays purposefully into the overall reason for their creation. You are supposed to work; you're not supposed to just job! Whoever told you to job?

Work is how we get out of us all that's inside of us. Dr. Myles Munroe says, "The true purpose of life is to live full and die completely empty!" You see, the reality is that all of us came to this earth *loaded* with gifts, talents, and abilities stored up inside of us. But it takes work—not a job, but work—to get what's inside of us out!

> Genius is one percent inspiration and ninety-nine percent perspiration.[28]
> —Thomas A. Edison

And once we get it out, the world benefits from it, and we fulfill what Mark Scharenbroich taught us in chapter 1 of this book. We leave this world better than the way we found it.[27]

Your Environment and Your Work

Even God worked. When God created this world, He worked for six days, and on the seventh day He rested. The first work assignment given to the first human being on the planet, Adam, was to name all of the animals on land and sea. God didn't give Adam a job; God put Adam to work. However, He put him to work in an environment where he was celebrated, he was capable, he was confident, he was challenged, and he was appreciated. That's where you should be. You should work in your own personal and professional Garden of Eden. I honestly believe that for each person with gifts and talents, there is an ideal environment where that person's gifts and talents flourish. And when we get our right gifts operating in the right place, then magic happens.

> When the social archaeologists of tomorrow look back on the days of yesteryear and find your footprint, what story will it tell? What social imprint will you make? What will your legacy be?
>
> —Jason Drenner

- Are you in the right place?

- Are you in the right environment for your best to come out of you?

- Are you in the place where you are celebrated and not just simply tolerated?

- Are you in a place where your creativity and imagination are encouraged daily?

- Are you in a place where you can do what you were meant to do?

Environment is critical to fulfillment and contentment. Seeds need the right environment of moist, nutrient-enriched soil and sunlight in order to grow into plants, vegetables, trees, fruits, flowers, and other vegetation. The seeds of your dreams need the same thing. They need the right environment and tools to create success. Now, just because you are in the right environment does not mean that things will be perfect. We all know that life comes with issues, challenges, disappointments, failures, and misfortunes. But I like to call all of those things the fertilizer that seeds need in order to grow to their fullest. So maybe you are not in the right environment at this present time, and maybe up until now, you have not produced the quality of life that is consistent with the best of what you really want for yourself and your family. The truth is you can't do anything about what was except learn from it and focus on creating a new version of what *is*!

Having the right gifts but being in the wrong place is not fun at all, because you still end up feeling frustrated. You still feel stuck, not because you are not using your correct talents and abilities, but because they are undervalued and/or underappreciated because they are in the wrong place. There is a perfect place for your gifts and talents to be developed and displayed, and I want to help you get there!

I remember hearing Zig Ziglar tell a story once that illustrates my point perfectly. It's an aeronautical fact that if you build a plane for an airline company and put it in a hangar, after a few years of not being utilized, the engine will be worn out! On the other hand, if you build a plane that is flown all over the country daily, the engine may need some service or routine maintenance, but that engine will be in much better shape than the one that did nothing in the hangar. The engine of a plane is wired, built, and engineered to be maximized at high altitudes. The valves, pistons, gaskets, fluids, oils, liquids, pumps, springs, motors, and other working/moving parts of the engine are all meant to function together, combined with the elements found only in high altitudes. Thus, without the right environment, the engine deteriorates. I have heard that the same is true of certain high-performance racing cars and boats. They must be driven often and at high speeds just to keep the engines from wearing out. I believe that the same is true for you. You must be in the right environment for your best to come out of you. Let me give you a few examples of what I am talking about.

> Far and away the best prize that life offers is the chance to work hard at work worth doing.[29]
>
> —Theodore Roosevelt

- Imagine Michael Jordan in a swimming pool rather than on a basketball court.

- Imagine Bill Gates selling cars rather than engineering the PC.

- Imagine Mel Gibson directing traffic rather than directing blockbuster movies.

- Imagine John Maxwell flying planes rather than writing and speaking on leadership.

- Imagine Albert Einstein building skyscrapers rather than teaching his genius to the world.

- Imagine Mary Kay Ash selling newspapers rather than founding Mary Kay Cosmetics.

- Imagine Donald Trump selling patio furniture rather than being a real estate mogul.

- Imagine Tiger Woods bagging groceries rather than winning PGA tours.

- Imagine Oprah Winfrey being a country singer rather than a TV broadcasting mogul.

- Imagine you . . .

You see, none of these people would have made the impact that they made and are still making on this world if they would have just settled for a working a job rather than working their dreams. The reality is that all the people we just mentioned, and millions of others whom we didn't, have had to pay the price of putting themselves in the right environments for their gifts and talents to blossom. Are you willing to pay that price?

THE ALMIGHTY DOLLAR

Why do we work? That's easy. Most people work for money.

- Money to live

- Money to take care of themselves and their families

- Money to save

- Money to spend

- Money to splurge

- Money to invest

- Money to save for a special occasion (i.e., wedding, newborn, family trip)

- Money to retire

- Money to contribute to other worthy causes

- Money to pay off debt

- Money to fund other worthwhile ventures

- Money to support their lifestyle of wants, needs, expectations, and wishes

Well, regardless of what we want to use the money for, everyone wants more of it! Everybody wants more money! Over the years, I have had the pleasure of meeting, coaching, speaking to, and developing tens of thousands of people, and one of the things that I hear most often is that people in the workplace, whether they like what they do or not, all want more money. They want more compensation for their perspiration.

There's nothing wrong with wanting more money; however, there is something wrong with wanting more output without evaluating and modifying the input. Most people don't put much into their work. That's why they don't get much out it. How can you take more money out of your bank account than you have deposited? It does not work that way unless you invest that money into a financial vehicle like an interest-bearing account designed to bring you a return

> We work to become,
> not to acquire.[30]
> —Elbert Hubbard

on that investment such as a mutual fund, money-market account, or IRA. The point is that we must put more of ourselves into our work so that we can get more (income, fulfillment, joy, and happiness) from our work.

The interesting thing is that we spend so much of our lives chasing the almighty dollar. However, many people have yet to learn that the very thing they are chasing is losing value the longer they chase it. That's why the most of the successful and financially prosperous people I know and have studied do not make the pursuit of money their primary motivating force in pursuing their life's work. Since they put meaning ahead of money, over time, money chased them down and still does to this day. In 1971 President Nixon took the U.S. dollar off the gold standard, and money became currency. According to Robert Kiyosaki's PBS special, when this happened, the U.S. government was then able to print currency faster than we could save it, which began to devalue the dollar.[31] And over the last thirty years, the dollar has lost 50 percent of its buying power!

In American society, we practically worship money! It's unfortunate but true.

Judging by our behavior, most people have an obsession with wealth. Turn on the television. You see game shows that teach us to play for large sums of money. You see infomercials that promise a "rags-to-riches" financial transformation if you buy a certain product. You also see reality shows that promise large sums of money to the winners. Unfortunately, you even see preachers who are using gimmicks and fancy marketing to coerce believers into giving beyond their means for hopes of healing and financial abundance. You see reality news shows centered around our fixation with Hollywood stars and celebrities who have money to burn. Politicians promise to create more of it while popular magazines are filled with gossip columns about those who have it, and the average person spends much of their adult life trying to obtain it. We are obsessed with money, and sadly, many of us are willing to cash in personal happiness, friends, and family in order to get it. However, most people have not learned that money only makes you more of what you already are! Money is a magnifier. If you're bad with five dollars, you'll be worse with five million dollars. However, if you are a giver with ten dollars, you'll be a philanthropist with ten million dollars. Again, money is a magnifier, and most people misunderstand it. They don't really know how to obtain it or how to hold on to it once they have it. In fact, 70 percent of the people that win the U.S. lottery (a once in a lifetime opportunity to create wealth) will go bankrupt three to five years after winning.[32]

Many people associate money with power, freedom, security, fulfillment, contentment, prestige, celebrity, opportunity, status, and wealth. Others associate money with greed, stinginess, stress, thievery, criminal misconduct, lack, scarcity, and poverty. But in reality, money is a tool. It's a resource. It's a vehicle to accomplish a goal. Most importantly, it's a mind-set. People who have money think differently than people who don't. Successful people think different thoughts than those who are consistently unsuccessful.

> **Your income is directly related to your philosophy, not the economy!**
>
> —Jim Rohn

As we learned in chapter 1, we spend one-third of our lives at this thing called work. Unfortunately, most people have a very negative view of work. That's because they have confused the joy of work with the drudgery of working a job they don't like. They view work as something that is a drag, a bore, a strain, and a bother when, in truth, work and your life's work was meant to be one of your greatest sources of joy and pleasure. I know many will argue that we just need more high-paying jobs, but I can also tell you, more money is not the problem! It's our philosophy and our approach toward the money we have that is the problem. The following is a great example that financial expert Larry Burkett used to share often in speeches to explain why more money is usually not necessarily the answer: "There's a man who makes $30,000 a year, one who makes $50,000, and another who makes $100,000. You probably think the first one may be getting by OK, the second one is doing a lot better, and the third one is doing great, right? Well, think again. When asked how they're getting along, they all usually say the same thing... 'We're just barely making ends meet!'"

Making ends meet. We all deal with it and try to succeed at it, but there is a big problem with working just to try to make ends meet. The problem is that every time we work to make ends meet, typically what happens is that those "ends" move! They get further and further apart. There are two reasons for this: (1) the ends move because we move them by spending more than we make and consistently living outside of our means, or (2) the ends move because of forces outside of our control.

> The definition of insanity is doing the same thing over and over, yet expecting a different result.
> —Author Unknown

First, let me say this to you: money should never be your primary motivating force for doing something, because money is only a temporary motivator! That's right. Although we make money every week or every two weeks, depending on how our payroll is set up, money is still a very temporary motivator. For most people, when they earn more, they typically spend more almost automatically. If someone starts off making $35,000 a year and then gets a huge promotion and starts making $50,000 a year, what typically happens is that person starts looking at society to ascertain what a $50,000-a-year lifestyle looks like in terms of clothes, cars, homes, and other extrinsic and commercially driven motivational forces. They then go out and upgrade their lifestyle to match the income level they have attained. It's called "keeping up with the Joneses."

There is nothing at all wrong with wanting nice things and wanting to live "high on the hog," but once a person spends equal to or in excess of what they earn, they experience a financial dilemma similar to Parkinson's Law, which states that "work expands so as to fill the time available for its completion." But when applied to money management, our *expenses* rise to meet income.

Your spending automatically increases to be consistent with your earning. Once this happens, the person making fifty thousand dollars is in the same financial situation they were in when they earned thirty-five thousand dollars. They immediately go back to living paycheck to paycheck, and the fifteen-thousand-dollar raise means nothing to them anymore. Simply because their income changed but their mind-set didn't, they repeated the same financially destructive behavior at a higher income level and got the same result. Additionally, now the primary motivator is not money, but rather the fear of what bills will not get paid if the money is not earned, thus a mind-set toward work is that, "All I do is work to pay bills!" And this is very frustrating.

The second challenge is fixed salary versus variable expenses! People who work for a set salary or wage have a fixed income. It does not change much unless overtime is worked or a bonus is given, but expenses are variable. In today's society almost everything is getting more and more expensive (variable) by the day. Most people who live on a fixed income with variable expenses wonder why they can't seem to make ends meet. It is almost a guaranteed losing battle also known as the "rat race." An attempt to offset this losing battle is called cost-of-living raises that take place each year as well as performance raises that reward good work with better pay, but often these 3–5 percent increases most people don't even really feel, especially after taxes. Remember, whenever you earn more in the wage and employee system, you will typically pay Uncle Sam more also. So consider a person making forty thousand dollars a year, which is fixed. Now look at that same person paying expenses every month that are variable:

- Food
- Rent
- Utilities
- Interest rates
- Mortgage
- Property taxes
- Entertainment
- Clothing
- Life insurance

- Gas
- Tuition
- Repairs
- Trips and vacations
- Car insurance
- Childcare
- Credit card debt
- Donations and giving
- Medical expenses

So again, the income is fixed, but the outgo is variable. Wouldn't it be great if when gas goes up fifty cents per gallon, your HR department calls you on the same day and gives you an instant fifty-cents-per-hour raise to make up for the expense? But we all know how unrealistic that is. It just does not happen. So how do we win? How do we get out of the rat race? We change our philosophy!

1. Instead of our income being fixed and our outgo being variable, we change it around so that our income is variable, and through budgeting and smart financial decisions, our outgo becomes more fixed.

   > When you change the way you look at things, the things you look at change!
   > —Wayne Dyer

2. We stop chasing money, and we start chasing meaning. We get very good at what we love to do—the thing that puts us into "flow state"—and we allow money to then chase us.

3. We start to think multiple streams of income. After all, if money can go out in multiple ways, then it needs to be able to come in via multiple ways.

4. We stop making others rich by depositing all of our greatness into other companies rather than investing in our own ventures.

5. We look at money as a reward for solving a problem! So we position ourselves as professional problem solvers, and we get paid to solve problems for people.

6. We begin to think abundance rather than scarcity and focus our attention and intention on attracting into our experience the fullness that is our right to attain.

Now look what you've done. You made me get ahead of myself. We will talk much more about these changes later on in the book. However, the essence is that we need to change the way we approach our work and our philosophy toward money. We need to stop jobbing and start dreaming!

THE THREE WAYS YOU CAN APPROACH WORK
(JOB, CAREER, CALLING)

While conducting my research for this book, I came across an article published by the Mayo Clinic Staff titled "Job Satisfaction: Strategies to Making Work More Gratifying."[33] A portion of that article stood out to me as foreground as it pertains to the three ways that most people approach the concept of work. According to the article, you can view your work as a job, career, or calling. The article goes on to give strategies for how you can add more meaning to your work based on the various ways you view your work. After reading that article, I created the following diagram to further illustrate the points in this book.

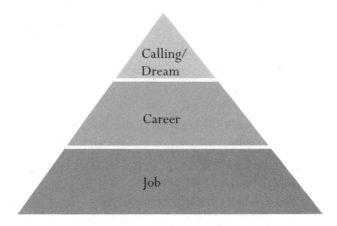

Take a good look at this diagram. I decided to use a pyramid or segmented triangle to illustrate the amount of people that typically pursue each approach and the amount of time we ultimately end up giving to each stage. I believe that most people approach work as a job—a simple exchange of time and effort for money and stability—and they spend a majority of their lives working in jobs. Those who have higher goals and ambitions approach work from the standpoint of establishing and growing more long-term careers. They pursued formal education and climbed this ladder of success after they got tired of the insecure job market. And lastly, those that want to achieve the highest level of success and fulfillment in life choose to move beyond jobs and careers into their lifetime calling and/or dream.

I believe that the ultimate place to arrive at in life—your "there"—is the place where you are doing what you were meant to do on this earth, and you've turned that into your livelihood. The only issue, as the diagram explains, is that for most people, by the time they finally reach their dream, they are older in years and have less time to enjoy that stage of life. In reality, that stage was available to them all along, but it took the right information, mind-set, associations, and the right actions to bring it forth. Few people really achieve this level of success, but it's available to everyone, and now through this book, I pray that you will embrace this level for yourself.

> **The tragedy of life is not that it ends so soon, but that we wait so long to begin it![34]**
>
> **—W. M. Lewis**

It is my hope, goal, and expectation that this book will make such a profound impact upon this world that a shift takes place in mankind and people spend less of their lives in jobs and careers and the majority of their lives living their calling and dreams, as the ideal diagram below represents.

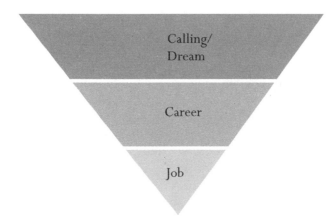

For the rest of this chapter, I will focus primarily on helping you understand the differences between the three approaches to work: job, career, and calling/dream, and the implications and opportunities associated with each one.

JOB

By now you should know how I feel about you approaching your work as just a job. If you approach work as a job, you are basically trading time and effort for money and stability; that's it. You probably have little to no real passion for your position; it's just something you do to meet the goal of getting a check. Your training to perform that job was probably minimal, and you typically feel like you're on autopilot when you do your job, because it has become stale, boring, and monotonous. Many people I've talked to use the word *robot* to best describe how they feel working their job. Well, let's look at the definition of the word *job*.

> **job** \ jăb \ *n* 1 : a piece of work or task done as
> part of one's occupation for an agreed price 2
> : a post of employment; full-time or part-time
> position 3 : anything a person is expected or
> obliged to do; duty; responsibility.

Interestingly, the very first definition of *job* is "a *piece* of work." So, in and of itself, a job isn't even full-blown work. It's a portion, a ration, a segment, or a fraction of work. It's a percentage of work. And millions of people every day cash in destiny, purpose, and their life's work for a fraction of work called a job. As I have interviewed thousands of people one-on-one, in small groups, and in large live audiences, I ask them what the top ten things that most people who work jobs feel. This is the feedback I get (in no particular order):

1. Stress
2. Fatigue
3. Frustration
4. Dissatisfaction
5. Boredom
6. Depression
7. Underappreciation
8. Overworked
9. Underpaid
10. Stuck

These are strong feelings, and I believe that all feelings, whether they are good or bad, serve us in some way. I believe that they communicate to us that our perspective and our focus is either right on or way off. Anthony Robbins states that there are approximately 6,000 different feelings that we have names for in the English language, and out of all those emotions, these were the top ten things, based on my research, that are felt by people who work in jobs.[35] Something is very wrong with this picture. Yet, this is the price that we pay when we settle for jobs rather than dreams! I am so glad you are reading this book.

In my estimation, I believe there are three types of jobs.

1. Dead-end jobs

Dead-end jobs have little to no upward or forward advancement. The pay is poor, the environment is demotivating, and the work itself is just not rewarding or fulfilling. If you have settled for this type of job, it's not fun to get up each morning, and my goal is help you get out of this type of job. It does not serve you. In order for you to transition into your calling and live the life you dream of living, you need room to grow and develop, and dead-end jobs don't provide opportunity for that. All they do is provide money—and maybe benefits.

2. Stepping-stone jobs

This is the type of job that is not permanent but is a good skill and experience builder for your future, while also providing you a paycheck. Stepping-stone jobs may have much or little to do with your ultimate calling or dream, but they are a vital part of your process and your journey. They are strategic. For example, I have been employed from the time I was four-teen years old, and I have never worked a dead-end job. All my jobs were stepping-stone jobs. Then I landed a dream job, which transitioned me into what I do now. However, each of the jobs I had in preparation for my calling and dream taught me important lessons in life and business that I still utilize today. I will teach more about those stepping-stone jobs in chapter 6. Ulti-mately, stepping-stone jobs are supposed to build upon one another and help you get to a place where transition can begin.

3. Dream jobs

Jobs that make possible the transition from job living to dream living are called dream jobs. They serve as the bridge or the connector from where you are to where you really want to ultimately be. We will talk much more about dream jobs in chapter 7. However, I will say this, the dream job is one of the most critical and transitional decisions you will ever make. Dream jobs are great, but they are very temporary. You have to use them wisely, or you could end up turning your dream job into a dead-end or stepping-stone job.

Many years ago, I heard one of my speaking mentors Willie Jolley tell a story of how he read in *USA Today* that a study was conducted of employers and employees in the workplace. The study confirmed that most employers paid employees just enough money so that they would not quit. The study also confirmed that most employees worked just hard enough for employers that they would not get fired. In between all of the "just enough" behavior, everybody ends up settling.

In the job world, you are mainly doing a task. That's why jobs, and sometimes even careers, are often so easily replaced with technology. We talked earlier about how corporations are now forced to compete for the best product, price, and service on a global scale. Since keeping you employed and making you financially prosperous is *not* the goal of most corporations, they will quickly replace you if technology advances enough to replace the tasks that you do manually. In the past, people looked to jobs for security and for a consistent paycheck. But now, with corporate downsizing, rightsizing, mergers, acquisitions, offshoring, and the like, even job security is becoming a joke in the real world.

Speaking of which, job offshoring is having a big impact on our American society and job economy. Donald Trump and Robert Kiyosaki both agree in their book, *Why We Want You to Be Rich*, that the middle class in America is shrinking, while the middle class in other foreign countries like India, China, and Japan is growing rapidly, and the reason is largely because of job offshoring and outsourcing.[36] Many colleges and universities are reporting dramatic declines in the number of students enrolling in management information systems, information technologies, and computer science degree programs. And in spite of the fact that the Bureau of Labor Statistics lists computer-related jobs in the top ten fastest growing and in-demand occupations between 2004 and 2014, job offshoring is giving young and seasoned professionals a moment of pause.[37]

Princeton economist Alan Blinder published a study in March 2007 on how many jobs might be at risk of being offshored or sent overseas in the next ten to twenty years. Here is a sample showing the wide range of categories that Blinder considers having a high potential for being offshored:[38]

POTENTIAL OFFSHORE JOBS	
Occupation	**Number of Jobs**
Computer programmers	389,090
Telemarketers	400,860
Computer systems analysts	492,120
Bookkeeping, auditing, and accounting clerks	1,815,340
Mathematicians	2,930
Actuaries	15,200
Film and video editors	15,200
Graphic designers	178,530
Medical transcriptionists	90,380
Architectural and civil drafters	101,040

This is only 10 of the 291 occupations that Blinder researched, but just from the list above, a total of 3,501,260 of these jobs could be offshored from the United States to other countries within the next ten to twenty years. Billions more were counted in this study.

Robert Kiyosaki is probably one of the most intelligent business minds that I know. I have been a student of his Rich Dad principles for many years now. I can remember when I read his *New York Times* best seller *Rich Dad, Poor Dad* for the first time.[39]

He mentioned in his book how people who get up each morning and go to a job just to make money to pay bills alone are in a financial rat race because they will never catch up. In the book, he states that the word *job* really stands for "just over broke." By "just over broke," Robert captured and harmonized the way that most people really and truly feel about their jobs. As we mentioned earlier, people work jobs to try to make ends meet, but because of overspending and variable expenses, those ends keep moving farther apart. Most people end up having more month at the end of their money instead of more money at the end of the month! It's a revolving cycle that is increasingly difficult to get out of. That's why so many financial gurus call it the rat race.

In an audio product of his called *Rich Dad's Guide to Becoming Rich...Without Cutting Up Your Credit Cards*, Robert Kiyosaki talks about the price of freedom versus security. He says that most people work jobs for the feeling of security that it gives them and their families, knowing that a steady paycheck is coming every two weeks. However, there is a time and place for that stability and security, but the price that one pays for that security is freedom. They don't get to take days off during the week, schedule their vacations when they want, wake up when they get done sleeping, or have the income freedom to make much more than their position pays. All of this freedom is the price that most people pay for security—the security of a paycheck that they have already outgrown!

> You will never discover new oceans until you have the courage to lose sight of the shore.
>
> —Author Unknown

On the other hand, the price that one must pay for freedom is security. And that is the price that most dreamers, inventors, entrepreneurs, great thinkers, and visionaries pay in order to live their calling and live their dreams rather than live a job! Many of them will admit that it was scary leaving the comfort of a good salary for the unknown possibilities of personal and professional freedom. However, once they took the leap, I don't know of one—not one—who has ever regretted it! A price must be paid either way, but to me, the price for freedom is a much better price to pay, and the rewards are a million times greater. The great thing about this book and this concept, however, is that I am going to teach you how to transition to your dream and keep both freedom and some level of security at the same time. You can have them both, but you just have to be willing to pay the price.

One of the greatest challenges with approaching your work as a job is that it sentences you to the wage system. According to Chris Widener on his audio program, *The Invisible Profit System*, there are only two income systems: the profit system and the wage system. I will talk more about the profit system in an upcoming section about your calling and dream. But I want to quickly address the pitfalls of working in the wage system. For sake of definition, the wage system is trading time for money. People that work jobs and careers typically earn an hourly wage or a fixed salary. Here are four problems with working in this system:

1. It puts a limit or a cap on how much you can earn.

2. Your income is completely determined by your effort and not the effort of others, so leveraging is not an option.

3. Your income can't increase without your income taxes increasing also.

4. You are a part of the highest taxed population of people in the United States because you are an employee.

Although there are a lot of good and bad jobs out there, approaching your work as a job is ultimately the worst decision you can make if you want to live the life you have always dreamed of.

CAREER

The next way that you can approach your work is by viewing it as a career. Have you heard the idea that singing is elongated speech? Well, careers are often elongated jobs. However, there are several key differences and distinctions that make careers a much more powerful dream step than just jobs. I like careers much more than jobs, and here are a few major reasons why.

> Wages make you a living; profits make you a fortune.
>
> —Author Unknown

1. Careers are more serious and long-term forms of employment than jobs.

2. Careers require more formal education and specialized training than jobs.

3. Careers tend to have better growth paths and development tracks than jobs.

4. Careers tend to offer more continuing education opportunities than jobs.

5. Careers have more professional associations and conferences dedicated to them, allowing people to network, share best practices, and sharpen one another.

6. Careers tend to offer much better benefit packages, perks, and bonus structures.

7. Careers provide skill sets and experiences that are highly transferable in the marketplace, making it easier to find future work if your situation changes.

8. Careers often allow a person to carve their unique position within a company.

9. Careers often offer much better pay scales and compensation plans overall.

10. Careers often allow for mentorship to take place within an organization.

11. Careers offer tenure, seniority, and other promotions that ensure job security.

12. Careers have the potential to become someone's calling or dream.

You can see that there are some marked differences between a job and a career, but the biggest difference is in the way you approach them. One person may call a position a job, and another person may call that same position a career. It can be the exact same position with the same hours, same pay, and same benefits, but the way each person approaches it and treats it will determine what they get out of it.

> **ca·reer** \ kuh-reer \ n 1 : an occupation or profession, esp. one requiring special training, followed as one's lifework 2 : a person's progress or general course of action through life or through a phase of life as in some profession or undertaking 3 : success in a profession, occupation, etc.

One of the nicest things about a career is that by definition it is an "occu-pation." It is something that you can jump into with both hands and get fully involved in. It's not a "piece of work" like a job, but rather it requires that you get engaged deeply within it. As we discussed earlier, many careers require years of specialized or formal training before you can begin them. A job is a task, but a career is a profession! Once you have a career, you move into the realm of being called a professional. The advancement path and track is so much better in careers than in jobs

> Paint a masterpiece
> daily. Always
> autograph your work
> with excellence.
> —Greg Hickman

because careers require more of an investment to attain them. They also tend to yield more perks and benefits.

Whatever you do in life, I believe that you were supposed to dominate it. Now when I say dominate, I don't mean in a negative, nasty, or cruel way. I mean in an empowering way that demonstrates your level of mastery of your profession. When you occupy something, you take a level of ownership in it. You can't drive a new car off the dealership lot until you purchase or lease it. Once you have taken some steps toward official ownership of the car, then you can occupy it fully. To fulfill the complete definition of *career*, you must occupy it.

```
oc·cu·py \ ok-yuh-pahy \ v 1 : to take or fill up
    (space, time, etc.) 2 : to engage or employ
    the mind, energy, or attention of 3 : to be a
    resident or tenant of; dwell in 4 : to take
    possession and control of (a place), as by
    military invasion 5 : to hold (a position,
    office, etc.)
```

Job is a noun; *career* is a noun; but *occupy* is a verb that means "action," and I like that. With a career occupation, we are to have a sense of ownership or vested interest in that position and in the organization within which we work. We bring our best to the organization because we know that by bringing our best, the company gets better because we are better. We come to work daily with an attitude that says, "I am the master of my career position, and I employ my mind, creativity, passion, and energy in a positive direction, which will create positive change!"

Now, as excited as I am about you approaching your work as a career, I must tell you that there are several challenges with careers and several commonalities between careers and jobs that still don't allow careers to be the final step of greatness that one can take. Careers, just like jobs, still keep you as an employee. They still keep you in the wage system, and they still can put a cap on how much growth you attain and income you earn. In both jobs and careers, someone else is still assigning a value to what they think you are worth.

Other challenges I see with careers:

1. Because of the formal education, time, and training invested to pursue a career, sometimes people get into careers and don't like them but feel a sense of loyalty to the career field because of all the prep work involved in getting there. This often keeps people doing well at the wrong job for five, ten, fifteen, or twenty years longer than they should have because of a sense of obligation.

2. Careers can sometimes be passed down through the family from one generation to the next. Some say this passing of the torch is very beneficial for those offspring who share the passion for the profession that their parents do, such as Don Trump and Ivanka Trump, the children of Donald Trump. Both work for him and love commercial real estate. However, for those kids who don't like the career path their parents chose, again because of a fear of disappointing their parents, that feeling of obligation and loyalty to the family business keeps many people stuck in a career they dislike or even hate.

3. Since careers still keep you in the wage system, careers can still suffer the same fate as jobs. They can be replaced by technology and innovation. Look at the music industry for instance. There are people who made their careers out of running music stores, and now with the introduction and explosion of the digital age, the power of downloads is forcing music stores to close left and right. The travel industry is another. Thousands of brick-and-mortar travel agencies have now closed their doors because of the new boom in Internet travel. Companies like YTB Travel and Cruises are changing the way people book and save money on travel. When you read in a newspaper that some big company let

go of one hundred thousand workers, not all of those people were working jobs. Many thousands were career professionals who had invested ten to twenty-plus years working for that organization. So careers can suffer the same fate as jobs.

4. Pursuing a career that you're not passionate about can cause serious financial debt. According to *USA Today* College Edition in 2005, 64 percent of college students in the United States used a student loan of some sort to earn their education. However, a sobering 75 percent of college students upon graduation took jobs and careers in fields that have nothing to do with their major in college. Young professionals are starting their careers off in tremendous amounts of debt because of bad career choices and major selections while in college.

> Get into a line of work that you will find to be a deep personal interest, something you really enjoy spending twelve to fifteen hours a day working at, and the rest of the time thinking about.
> —Earl Nightingale

In spite of these challenges, millions of people have proven that careers can be a very rewarding and fulfilling aspect of life, as long as the career is connected somehow to what they ultimately see as their life's calling or dream.

CALLING/DREAM

I could have easily called this book *Caught Between a Calling and a Job*, because the words *calling* and *dream* have the same meaning. Many people find that the term *calling* is more synonymous or consistent with the spiritual community or religious crowd. And while that may be true in some circles, the term *calling* is really just that inner knowing of what you were really meant to do with your life. It's that awakening to the you that you've always been and wanted to be. Your calling or dream is the ultimate fulfillment of your life's purpose working in perfect harmony with your professional occupation.

```
call·ing \ kaw-ling \ n 1 : the act of a person
    or thing that calls 2 : vocation, profession,
    or trade 3 : a call or summons 4 : a strong
    impulse or inclination
```

I will be spending the rest of this book helping you tap in to your calling and dream and showing you how you can begin the process of transitioning strategically from where you are to where you really want to be. Since the rest of this book is dedicated to your calling and dream, I am not going to spend a lot of time here talking about it, but allow me to underscore a few key benefits of living your calling and your dream.

1. Living your dream will more than likely require that you start some form of business.

2. When you become your own boss, you determine your worth; it's not assigned to you, which means that your income potential is unlimited.

3. When you live your calling, the work that you do does not feel like labor. It's fun.

4. You enter into the profit system where you earn profits and not just wages.

5. Your time is maximized because you are now investing it into the deepest hopes, dreams, and desires that you have. You take your life more seriously, and things blossom faster.

6. You can't be fired, downsized, offshored, or right-sized from your dream. It's yours!

7. Having your own business is one of the only legal tax shelters left in America today. As an entrepreneur, you can typically earn more money and pay less in taxes than an employee.

8. Talk about freedom and opportunity. You have so much of both in your dream.

I am a strong proponent of approaching work as a calling and dream. Now, I know what you are thinking: "Isn't there risk involved?" Yes, but look at all you risk by not going for your dream. I believe that command reveals potential. In other words, if you feel that either God told you to pursue your dream or you hear something deep inside you constantly telling you that you are more than what you have become, then I believe that the command to do it proves that you are capable of achieving it. If you believe it, you can achieve it!

In closing, I would like to share a story with you. It is a true story of someone who, despite the odds, was willing to pursue her greatness and the greatness of those she served, and in doing so, she is now living her calling and dream. Her story powerfully illustrates the difference between approaching work as a job, a career, and a calling or dream!

In the movie *Freedom Writers*, Erin Gruwell graduated from California State University with a degree in education and headed to Wilson High School to begin her career as a freshman English teacher.[41] In college she actually started out studying law but changed her mind, switched majors, and pursued education. Erin had no idea how difficult her first teaching opportunity would be when she was given a classroom full of students whom the educational system had deemed "unteachable" and "at risk." Her students—all of which were minority students except one and all of which had firsthand exposure to gang violence, juvenile detention, drugs, crime, and poverty—were prepared to eat Erin for lunch each day. However, by fostering an educational philosophy that valued and promoted the appreciation of diversity, she transformed room 203 into a sanctuary for her students to learn, think critically, shatter stereotypes, rechart their futures, journal their pain and pleasures, and ultimately create a family.

> The self-employed are the wealthy folks of America. The average net worth of a family where the head of a household works for someone else is $65,000. When it comes to the self-employed, the average net worth is $352,300.[40]
>
> —Dr. Steve Sjuggerud

Fighting an uphill battle to try to get her students the types of learning materials, resources, books, and field trips that would expose them to a new way of thinking and believing, Erin was often turned down by the superiors for these types of quality resources. Determined to provide them anyway, she took a few jobs on the side to earn extra money to fund the needs of her students. She worked at a lingerie shop and a hotel to generate the extra revenue needed to fund the calling that she felt deep within her for her students' success. In a matter of a few short years, Erin was able to transform a group of one hundred fifty "at-risk" students into graduating seniors who were all college-bound! She took the stories of the students and helped them turn their experience into a book called *The Freedom Writers Diary*. She furthered her teaching career by accepting a Distinguished Teacher in Residence position at her alma mater, CSU–Long Beach. Additionally, she is now living her dreams and fulfilling her calling as the president of the Freedom Writers Foundation.[42]

The human mind is the last great, unexplored continent on earth. It contains riches beyond our wildest dreams, and it, like fertile farmland, will return to us, anything we want to plant.[43]

—Earl Nightingale

Stop. Think about what all this means. She earns wages through the university, high wages I am sure, but she is also the head of her own foundation, which puts her in the profit system. She is also a successful author of the book *Teach With Your Heart* and is a high-demand keynote speaker at corporate, educational, government, and community conferences and conventions nationwide. *Stop again.* Now she is really making major profits from consulting, keynote speeches, book sales, CD sales, private coaching, and movie deal rights. I'd like to see someone offshore, downsize, or right-size that. They can't. Why? Because she built this through her ultimate calling and dream, which she can never be fired from.

So let's recap here. She took ownership of her career occupation as a teacher. She used jobs as a side-dish means to fund her heart's desires in her career. While working in her career, she realized that her gifting and purpose lay in helping special students overcome their issues and pursue their greatness. She then launched books and other dream opportunities, which were so compelling that it attracted the attention of Paramount Pictures, who turned her story into a blockbuster movie named after her students, *Freedom Writers*! Now, consider how one woman against the odds was able to accomplish all of this and still continue to grow her calling and dream. Let me ask you a question that I have asked you a few times throughout this chapter: whoever told you to job?

CHAPTER SUMMARY

EIGHT POINTS TO PONDER
DURING YOUR TRANSITION

1. Remember that you will typically work eighty-three thousand hours throughout your life. So choose to live abundantly rather than simply existing efficiently.

2. Choose to frame your work around your life and not your life around your work, and especially not around a job.

3. The job satisfaction statistics paint a very ugly picture of the realities of the current workforce environment, so make a choice now to change your destination.

4. There are four ages that mankind has lived through that have changed the way we work: the hunter/gatherer age, the agricultural age, the industrial age, and the information age. Now we are embarking upon the fifth, the creative age.

5. Realize that you must—and I do repeat, must—be in the right environment for your best to come out of you.

6. Stop chasing money, and start chasing meaning. Pursue your dreams and your greatness because it is your responsibility, not because it will make you rich. Remember, money is only a temporary motivator.

7. There are three ways that you can approach your work: as a job, as a career, or as a calling/dream. Additionally, realize that your approach can change and evolve as you change and evolve.

8. Remember that you were meant to work, not job! So choose to work your dreams and not a job, and you will experience abundance and freedom beyond your wildest dreams.

CHAPTER 3

MY STORY: A LIFE BY DESIGN

Getting fired is nature's way to telling you that you had
the wrong job in the first place.[1]

—Hal Lancaster

CONGRATULATIONS! YOU HAVE MADE IT THUS FAR, AND I AM SURE THAT by now your brain is going a hundred miles an hour if not on overload. That's a good thing. In this chapter, though, I am going to shift gears a little and take you back. I want to give you some insight into myself and my background. I want to share a brief part of my story and show you where my work ethic came from. I will share with you several of the critical change points in my life and what I learned during those change points that helped me to become who I consistently evolve into being.

HUMBLE BEGINNINGS

As I travel this world impacting people's lives through motivation and empowerment, I am often asked this powerful question: what was it that made you want to get into professional speaking? Some people ask because they themselves are interested in becoming speakers, and many others ask because they think that it is such a neat field of work to be involved in. Scary, some say, but neat! In all my years, I have never heard someone say, "It must be hard to be you and to do what you do for a living!" I am proud to say that I am very blessed and honored to do what I do for a living. Each morning that I wake up, I know that someone's life will change for the better because of something that has my sweat equity in it.

As long as I can remember, I have been a fan of wisdom. I have always been drawn to intelligent people, places, things, mind-sets, and the like. My passion for wisdom began with quote books. From as young as I can remember, I was always impressed with brainy, witty, profound, intellectual, and purposeful one-liners, catch phrases, and quotes. Quotes on all subjects—love, spirituality, knowledge, destiny, enterprise, business, relationships, nature, the meaning of life, and so on. I was always drawn to people who had the ability to communicate in a way that people could relate to. I was born and raised in the church, and although I was like most kids who went to sleep during the sermons, when I was awake, I found myself drawn and compelled by the way that preachers were able to convey their ideas with such passion and inspiration. I was enamored with the way that certain ministers could tell profound stories and use illustrations, metaphors, and vivid language to paint powerful portraits in the minds and hearts of the congregation. However, with all of that impression, I never felt a calling from God to become a preacher or pastor. Nor did I feel that such a calling would be my ultimate destiny, so I had to find an alternative.

I began to read inspirational books and watch television, and I found myself drawn to movies, shows, and documentaries that were inspiring and that had a success or motivational flair to them. Even when I would watch regular movies, I would somehow see and discover various inspirational elements in the movies that really compelled me to think critically about how that lesson in that movie could benefit others. So much so that now, in many of my keynote presentations, I incorporate movie clips to support my points. All of this began for me as a child, watching movies like *Rocky*, *Indiana Jones*, *The Lion King*, and a host of others. This began my journey of discovery into the world of motivation and empowerment.

My mother, Olivia B. McNeal, is a huge motivational force behind who I am today. My mom raised my brother, Michael T. McNeal, and myself with tremendous loving care and standards of excellence that were nonnegotiable. My mother is a powerful orator in her own right, and she taught me from a very early age about the power of speech and oral communication. I can remember the very first speech I ever gave. It was in church when I was seven years old. I was asked to recite Matthew 1:21 as my part in a Christmas play. My mom practiced with me at home and in the car and helped me with memorization, diction, articulation, projection, direction, stage presence, and eye contact. When the day came to recite the verse, I stepped out in front of the anxious yet supportive congregation at St. John Progressive Missionary Baptist Church, and I confidently delivered my first speech. My mom confirmed how well I did with a huge hug, kisses, and compliments all the way home. From that day forth, I started getting the longest parts in the Easter and Christmas plays rather than the short ones. And because my brother Michael and I were "Olivia's sons," we were targets for any and all church activities that involved speaking. Her legacy had paved the way for us, and if my mother had not become who she was, I would not be who I am, and you probably would not be reading this book right now.

My mother and father divorced when I was two, so for about four and a half years, my mom was a single mom raising two boys. We moved from Tampa to Tallahassee, where my mother worked as the director of vocational training at Florida A&M University. We lived in a cool apartment in a nice neighborhood full of kids my age. My mother raised both Michael and me with a strong work ethic. She gave us responsibilities around the house to take care of and gave us rewards when we did our part. She made sure that we had whatever we needed to be successful in school, although during that time, I was not really taking school all that seriously. Mom says that I used to practice bad handwriting just to

> It only takes a minute
> to change your life.[2]
>
> —Willie Jolley

frustrate her. I was a very curious child, and from what my scholarship warnings used to say, I was very talkative. In my early years in school, I made decent grades but low marks for conduct because I was always trying to get attention.

Pause!

Now let's think about this for a second. I was a little kid with tremendous gifts inside me even then, but I was using my gifts for the wrong reason. I was confident enough to be talkative, but I wasn't saying much of anything! You see, I believe that many of our youth today begin displaying the talents early in their development that they will ultimately be rewarded for. If we nurture and develop those gifts and talents rather than being so quick to label them as "at risk" or "hyperactive," then those talents can grow into abilities and skills for effective use in the marketplace.

Back to the story.

ME AND MS. D

After enough lectures, prayers, and spankings, I finally started getting my act together academically. We moved back to Tampa roughly a year before I started the sixth grade. My entire life changed, however, when I met Diane Williams. Ms. D, as she is affectionately known, was my sixth grade teacher at Progress Village Elementary School. Because of my not-so-great academic performance in the fifth grade, I was placed in a precautionary class for "at-risk" students in the sixth grade. Ms. D did not play, and to this day, she does not play! She came into that classroom on the first day and told me, "Son, you are not a youth at risk. You are a youth with a promise!" She immediately relabeled me and told me that she would not allow me or anyone else in that class to settle for less than excellence in their academics! She was not impressed with my antics, jokes, or comedy. She saw right through my pleasant but over-the-top attitude and chopped me down to reality.

> The best way to predict the future is to create it.[4]
>
> —Peter Drucker

She and my mother formed a bond and double-teamed me to make me straighten up and fly right. I can honestly say that my entire life changed because of the dynamic duo of my mother and Ms. Diane Williams. They formed a partnership and would not allow me to perform below the best of what I was capable. I felt like I had two moms—one at home and one at school. Then if I count the ones I had at church, I realize I was never without guidance, direction, and encouragement.

Once my academics improved, I was able to get into the performing arts, sing in chorus, and play bongos in the band. I won school talent shows, and I even developed leadership abilities by being selected as a bus patrol. All of this change took place within the span of one school year. Change does not take long if your reasons are compelling enough!

My mother and Ms. D helped me to connect my gifts and talents with a greater purpose in life. They showed me how my gifts would be celebrated if utilized in the right environments. They taught me to never try to compete against others but always to catch up with the vision that I see of myself in my future. Together they made me realize that I could be popular and productive at the same time. After the sixth grade, I didn't have any more academic challenges. I realized that doing well in school made my mother proud, caused her less stress, and gave me more opportunities. Finally, I learned that I could create my future based on my present behavior. These were powerful lessons to learn at such a young age.

Default Versus Design

I believe with all of my heart that life gives us various choices. These choices are not always easy, but they are certainly always necessary. One such choice is how we will live our lives. I believe that you can live your life by default or by design. I just recently heard of this term *default versus design* in 2006 from a gentleman by the name of Dr. Robert Anthony. My life took an incredible turn for the better in 2006 when a good friend of mine turned me onto a powerful teaching by Dr. Robert Anthony. He's a behavioral psychologist, an NLP practitioner, a personal performance trainer, and the author of over fifteen books. He created the audiobook series called The Secret of Deliberate Creation.[4] In that audio program, he speaks of this concept in great detail. I would like to expound on the concept in my own words from the standpoint of the fact that I have used this mind-set of designing my life for over a decade now. If you are going to transition your life from jobbing to dreaming, then you have to stop defaulting your life and start designing it with intention.

> **You must customize in order to maximize!**
>
> **—Delatorro L. McNeal II**

In chapter 2 we talked about the difference between people that exist versus those who live. How we choose to live our lives—either by default or by design—greatly influences that. If we live by default, we will exist efficiently, but if we live by design, we will live abundantly. The sixth grade was such a huge changing point for me because I really internalized the fact that I could actively play a role in creating my future. I finally awoke to the reality that I could dictate my tomorrow based on my actions or inactions today.

And the same is true of you. Think about the average computer. When you first buy a computer from the store, that computer comes loaded with certain software, and it also has hardware built into it. The computer also comes with many features and functions preset by the manufacturer at what's called "default settings." These settings are basic levels that the creator and producer of the product programmed into the device for minimal peak performance. However, the manufacturer fully expects for the customer, or the end user (which is you and me), to change many of the settings on the computer to better match our specific needs. In other words, the manufacturer expects that the customer will change the default settings to optimize and maximize the product.

For example, I am a Mac lover. I used to be a PC lover for many years, but as I got more into presentations and multimedia, my dear friend Jason took me into an Apple store one day, and I have been hooked ever since. Well, when I first purchased my Mac laptop, I did not know how to operate it, so I set up a ProCare appointment with a technician. He spent an entire hour showing me how to customize and design my Mac my way. There were features that, as a professional speaker, I needed turned on, but by default, they came turned off by the manufacturer. There where other features that, as a mobile professional, I wanted turned off, but they came in the default settings from the manufacturer as turned on. Now imagine how unproductive I would be on my Mac if I did not invest the time and effort into customizing and designing my Mac to my preferences. But amazingly enough, people go through life—a life that was meant to be full of customization—with the same ol' factory settings they were born with.

Just the other day, I was listening to some music on iTunes. The song was nice, but it sounded much different on my computer than it did in my car. So I called one of my techie friends over who is really good with that kind of stuff to see why there was a discrepancy between the car and the computer. After listening to it himself, he told me that my problem had an easy solution. He went into my preferences in iTunes and changed my EQ settings. All

> Pray as though everything depended on God. Work as though everything depended on you.[5]
> —Saint Augustine

of a sudden, that same song came to life in a completely new way. Now, all my songs sound as good on my laptop as they do in my car. And just think, for all that time, I was missing out on the beauty of all of my music being played with better EQ just because I had not taken the time to change the default settings.

I believe with all my heart that you and I are supposed to customize this thing called life and this thing called work to fit us best. I hear people say this next statement all the time, and I totally disagree with it. They say, "Life is not like Burger King; you can't have it your way!" I think that is absolutely untrue! You *can* have life your way. Now, that does not mean that things in life will always go your way 100 percent of the time, but it does mean that you can design your life to be whatever you want. You are the Michelangelo of your life, and you are in charge of painting your own masterpiece with the gifts, talents, abilities, resources, time, and opportunities that God blesses all of us with every day.

People who believe that Burger King quote wait for life to hand them situations, circumstances, and dilemmas, then they react and play the victim and wonder why they don't have the quality life they want. As long as you are waiting for things to happen to you, you are just taking life as it comes. Instead of waiting for promotions, why not give yourself a promotion? Instead of waiting for someone to hire you, why don't you hire yourself? People who live by default are reactive, whereas people who live life by design are proactive. And that's what you want to be.

From a product standpoint, the word *default* means "standard, average, common, regular, basic, and ordinary." Now, place any of those words in front of your life, and tell me that you want to settle for that. I rarely meet people who want—as their highest goal in life—standard success, average relationships, common goals, regular pay, basic friendships, and ordinary opportunities. Instead, I meet tons of people who want significant success, incredible relationships, superior goals, sensational pay, genuine friendships, and extraordinary opportunities. To get this, it will take some customization on your part. Understand that life will not just hand you this by default. Instead, you must achieve this by deliberate design.

> A ten-thousand-dollar life by design is worth more than a one-million-dollar life by default!

When you design your life, you create the terms. A designed life, I will admit, requires some work, but so does a default life. So in my estimation, you might as well go for the one that will bring you and your family the most joy. And you must be disciplined in order to get it. I once heard Zig Ziglar say, "You must be willing to do what you've gotta do until you get to do what you want to do."

Early in my life, I decided that I would work a few jobs on the way to my dream and that I would design my life and be intentional about the relationships. Your family is connected to you by default, but your friends are connected to you by design. You are stuck with your family, but you can change and choose your friends. Choose wisely! I learned way back in the sixth grade that I would become just like the folks I spend a lot of time with. So even back then, I decided to design my friendships around people who were going somewhere positive. You should be doing the same. I decided to be tough on myself so that life would be easier on me. I chose to design each day with things that brought me joy, and I chose to live my life as a designer and a creator.

Once you become a dream-life designer instead of an ordinary-existence defaulter, everything changes for you. Once you embrace the fact that you are made in the image and likeness of the Master Designer, then you start walking in your own designs as well. Your entire life becomes a life that you have designed.

> We must all suffer from one of two pains: the pain of discipline or the pain of regret. The difference is discipline weighs ounces while regret weighs tons.[6]
> —Jim Rohn

- You design your friendships and associations.

- You design your business partnerships.

- You design your entrepreneurial ventures and multiple-income streams.

- You design your income, and you determine how much you want to earn.

- You design your occupational title and call yourself what you choose.

- You design your family life and the quality time needed to support it.

- You design your learning and your development.

- You design your ability to give back and contribute to things you believe in.

- You design your time. (So you can actually go to the movies during the week. What a concept!)

- You design how you will raise your children.

- You design the type of legacy you want to leave behind.

- You design your spiritual growth and development.

You are an amazing designer original, my friend. Once God made you, the mold was broken, and He stamped your hands with a special pattern just to constantly remind you that you are the one and only. Your responsibility now becomes to design yourself a life that you love and enjoy—a life where you get to master your gifts and talents and utilize them to serve others.

You Are a Professional Problem Solver

I can remember attending a Wisdom Breakfast at the Marriott Hotel in 2003 in Tampa, Florida. There were business professionals, entrepreneurs, ministers, pastors, and members of the general public who all came together to glean wisdom from one of the wisest men that I have studied for years. His name is Dr. Mike Murdock, and without question, I believe that he is one of the most profound teachers of motivational thought today. On this particular day, he was sharing many principles for success in life, business, ministry, and personal development. One of the most powerful statements that he made was the fact that we are all professional problem solvers (PPS). Now, on the surface, that sounds pretty simple, but after you let it sink in, it gets really deep. He went on to explain that once a person embraces the fact that he is a PPS, then the way he goes about living his life completely changes because of the following four realities:[7]

> You were born a priceless original; don't you dare die a cheap copy.

1. A PPS understands that he was put on this earth with gifts and talents that were meant to unlock potential for others.

2. A PPS understands that the gifts and talents that were given him must be developed, cultivated, and mastered to be best utilized.

3. A PPS understands that he can make a job, a career, but most of all a calling/dream out of simply utilizing his mastered gift to solve problems for others.

4. A PPS understands that his phone rings predominately when there is a problem that his gifting solves, so he focuses his life on mastering the gift he is called for the most.

Now, what's interesting is that although I did not learn this lesson from Dr. Murdock until I was in my midtwenties, when I look back over my life, I realized that I have been solving problems for organizations all of my working life. I saw how I gravitated toward jobs and career opportunities that were aligned with my natural gifts, talents, personality, and abilities. I also learned that each one of these stepping-stone jobs led to greater opportunities and taught me many lessons about life and business that I still use today. And you know what? I bet the same is true of you, too.

MY TRANSITION FROM THE WAGE SYSTEM TO THE PROFIT SYSTEM AND WHAT IT CAN TEACH YOU

To further communicate this point, I would like to walk you through the jobs that I have had from the time I was fourteen years old until I was twenty-six. You see, I spent twelve years in the wage system, but during that entire time, I was building myself into the person that I needed to be to transition into the profit system. Now, everything I do is 100 percent in the profit system and will be for the rest of my life. I had ten jobs and two brief career positions before I transferred to the profit system. As I share with you each stepping-stone job, I will tell you briefly about my duties and what I learned from that job to help me be the CEO of several companies that I am today. Then I will ask you what jobs you have had that taught you some of the skills that I learned. Please use this section to take notes about your own life.

Stepping-stone job one: package executive, Winn-Dixie Stores

You all know what a package executive is, right? Well, it was my job to secure the safe transfer of purchased items from the store to the client's motor vehicle in such an ergonomic fashion. I was a *bag boy*! This is what I mean by how you can approach work. This was not a dead-end job to me. I saw this opportunity as a stepping-stone to my calling and dream. I worked there for exactly two years, and I was the best package executive they ever had. I was promoted to head package executive and trained and supervised fourteen other package executives during my two-year tenure with Winn-Dixie.

Lessons learned: responsibility, organization, customer service, training and development skills, leadership, and financial stewardship

What job/career taught you these skills?

_____

_____

Most people think that an "entry-level" and "menial" job such as bagging groceries surely can't yield these lessons, but I would beg to differ. When I was fourteen, I was listening to a Zig Ziglar tape, and he said, "Always outperform your paycheck, because if you do more than you are paid to do, the day will come when you are paid more for what you do!" That stuck with me, and I've applied it ever since that day. I have lived by that adage, and it has served me incredibly well for many years. In fact, I am living proof that it's true. When I was bagging groceries, I was making $4.75 per hour. But I did a lot more than $4.75 an hour paid me for. Now, as a professional speaker, I earn more in one hour speaking than the average American earns in a month! I am not telling you that to impress you but rather to impress upon you a principle: not all compensation comes in the form of a check. Many times it shows up in your character! Profound!

Stepping-stone job two: custodial executive, St. John Progressive Missionary Baptist Church

I worked as a sanitation engineer (janitor) for two years with my older brother Michael and my now-deceased stepfather. I learned the true meaning of working at a church. I performed many very humbling tasks around the church to keep it in top shape for ministry.

Lessons learned: teamwork, order, respect for authority, and quality

What job/career taught you these skills?

_____

_____

Stepping-stone job three: sales consultant, Service Merchandise

I was a sales consultant in the sight and sound department of the store and sold electronics for two years while in transition from high school to my early days in college. I learned a lot about teamwork, selling with integrity, and the importance of customer relationships.

Lessons learned: teamwork, time management, goal setting, sales, and service

What job/career taught you these skills?

_____

_____

Stepping-stone job four: management intern, Circuit City

I worked as a manager-in-training for four months at two separate stores. I wore the red jacket that managers wore but had no real authority to make major decisions. I worked in stock, inventory, HR, payroll, and direct customer sales.

Lessons learned: integrity, employee appreciation, interview skills, and money management

What job/career taught you these skills?

_____

_____

Stepping-stone job five: orientation leader, Florida State University (FSU) Office of Orientation

This was my dream summer job as a college student. I worked alongside thirty-five other student leaders at FSU to conduct summer orientation for approximately fourteen thousand students and parents. This was student leadership at its finest. I loved this job.

Lessons learned: team building, public speaking, leadership, accountability, and mentorship

What job/career taught you these skills?

_____

_____

Talk about change points! While I was in college, I was determined not to use a student loan to earn my education. I was blessed with a few partial academic scholarships, and because my father, Delatorro L. McNeal Sr., was a Vietnam War hero, I was able to get benefits through the VA. However, even with all of this, I still had bills, books, and standard of living expenses to take care of. My position as an orientation leader at Florida State was the funniest and most life-changing experience that I had in college. I developed my passion for leading people and for speaking to large groups of people. I literally fell in love with speaking motivationally to large groups through this position. I met tons of students and parents, and I got to see how Florida State played such a key role in the dreams of the students who wanted to go there. The pay was not that great, but I had free room and board over the summer, plus I got college credit for it!

Stepping-stone job six: peer advisor, FSU College of Communication

This was a great college job for my major. I worked in the dean's office for two years while I was earning my BA degree. As a peer advisor, I worked with freshman and sophomore students who wanted to get into the College of Communication. I gave registration advice to students on the best classes to take.

Lessons learned: access to educational professionals, networking, the power of recommendation, gatekeeping, mentorship, counseling, and peer support

What job/career taught you these skills?

_____

_____

**Stepping-stone job seven: resident assistant,
South Gate Campus Center, FSU**

In this position, I was in charge of the fifth-floor residents for one year and one summer term. I worked with a team of twelve other RAs to maintain the building and make sure that the residents behaved and had all their needs met. Free room and board made this job perfect for me.

Lessons learned: appreciation for diversity, leadership, teamwork, conflict resolution, peer counseling and advising, and mentorship

What job/career taught you these skills?

_____

_____

**Stepping-stone job eight: graduate assistant,
FSU College of Education**

I landed this job opportunity my first semester of graduate school at Florida State. I worked in the dean's office and served in multiple capacities as needed by higher administration in the College of Education.

Lessons learned: the power of relationships, work ethic, how to be mentored, being specific about my future, vision, entrepreneurship, and multitasking

What job/career taught you these skills?

_____

_____

Stepping-stone job nine: instructional design intern, W. D. Dick and Associates

I had multiple jobs in grad school so that I could graduate without taking out a student loan. This internship helped to hone my skills in the instructional design industry (which is what I have a master's degree in), while teaching me the business of being an independent contractor.

Lessons learned: "Fake it till you make it," partnership, entrepreneurship, diversity, client relationships, networking, family support, teamwork, and delayed gratification

What job/career taught you these skills?

Stepping-stone job ten: organization and human performance analyst, Andersen Consulting

This was my big corporate career position after graduate school. I learned so much about myself and about corporate America during this season of my life. It was my plan to work there for ten years and then slowly transition into speaking full-time, but you already know that's not what happened. I was released from this job unexpectedly and forced out of my comfort zone. But my layoff became my layup for my slam dunk! And you would not be reading this book right now had I not been let go. I turned my setback into a comeback, and you can do the same!

> If life knocks you down, that's not your fault. But if I come back a week later, and you are still on the ground...that's your fault!
>
> —Al Sharpton

Lessons learned: the high life, politics, the good ol' boy network, the School of Hard Knocks, travel, client relationship management, leadership, integrity, consistency, character, loneliness, career versus calling, the power of networking, and entrepreneurship

What job/career taught you these skills?

Without question, getting fired from my first corporate career position was the biggest change point in my professional career. Considering that my company and its sister company had just split and massive corporate layoffs were taking place all over the company, I was not very surprised by the termination. Several of my friends from graduate school suffered the same fate. Mine just came at a very bad time, because two months prior to getting terminated, I closed on my first house. I was just getting used to making my new house payments when the floor dropped out from underneath me, and I had a choice to make. I could either sink or swim. So I started flappin'!

> Faith is a knowledge within the heart, beyond the reach of proof.[8]
>
> —Kahlil Gibran

When presented with a major challenge, issue, or painful situation in life, you can do one of two things: allow that situation to make you bitter or allow that situation to make you better. It's not about what happens to you; it's about what happens *in* you that counts! And I know that hindsight is twenty-twenty, but even as I was going through that rough situation, deep down inside I knew that my calling and dream was much higher than that corporate career position. My time there was short and to the point, and I learned a lot from that experience. I believe that life often forces us into directions that many times we may not have found ourselves! Allow everything in your life—good, bad, ugly, or indifferent—to make you better.

THE ART OF ALLOWING

When was the last time you really, and I mean really, allowed yourself to want what you really want out of life? One of my mentors, Dr. Lee Jones, used to give a speech titled "You Must Give Yourself Permission." In that speech he used to talk about this very concept called the art of allowing. I believe that "allowing" is a true art form. Some people are masters of it while others can barely get themselves in the vicinity of real allowing. The reason I bring this up is because at this point in my life, I had to really allow myself to see the possibility of pursuing my full-time speaking dream as a reality. I had to permit myself to dream that far and see myself as a young speaker, still making a great impact and a great income to support my new family. My immediate reaction to the layoff was that I would just go out and get a new career position with another big-time consulting firm like Andersen. However, I had to allow myself to see beyond the wage system and into the glorious future of the profit system. I had to allow myself to see myself as an employer, not just an employee. And if I didn't allow what I knew was deep within me to come forth, my companies would not exist. My four books before this one would not exist, and I know with 100 percent accuracy that I would not be nearly as fulfilled and content as I am today. I had to believe in a dream that only I could see. And so must you. I had to trust in myself and in my God enough to know that if I mastered and marketed my gifting well enough, someone would buy it! If I promoted myself as a professional problem solver of motivational and empowerment problems to people and organizations that had those problems, I would get paid to solve problems! I had to have faith in myself, in my dream, and in my ability to make my dreams come true, regardless of my age and stage in life. And so must you.

In the movie *The Karate Kid, Part III*, Daniel-San, as Mr. Miyagi called him, was in the final round of competition for the belt. His opponent was killing him, and an illegal blow sent Daniel-San to the mat, struggling just to catch his breath. Mr. Miyagi, his teacher and mentor, rushed out to give him a few words of encouragement. However, Mr. Miyagi couldn't get a word in edgewise because Daniel-San was complaining, crying, and demanding to go home and to just quit the fight. Mr. Miyagi finally gets Daniel's attention with a loud "Ohyi." He says to Daniel-San, "OK to lose to opponent. Never OK to lose to fear." Daniel-San interrupts and says, "I'm afraid! I'm afraid of this guy! What am I supposed to do about it?" Mr. Miyagi tells his student, "Use focus. Your best karate still inside. Now time let out!"[9] And with that, Mr. Miyagi walked off the mat and went back to his post.

Daniel-San pondered the thought for several seconds while the audience and his opponent screamed, cheered, booed, and clapped. Daniel-San allowed Mr. Miyagi's advice to go

> **Your mint is hidden behind your meant.**
> —**Delatorro L. McNeal II**

deep into his heart, and he acted on the advice. Daniel-San beat his opponent with the simplest of karate moves and won the match, all because he allowed what was already inside of him to just come out. Mr. Miyagi did not have to teach Daniel anything new. He just had to inspire Daniel to look past his pain and focus on his innate ability!

See, here is the reality. No matter how great you are, whatever is inside of you will do no good and be no benefit to anyone until you *allow* what is in you to come out! I believe that you know that you are a person of greatness! But now it's a matter of you allowing yourself to want what you really want, to see the fullness of your greatest dreams, to act intelligently and consistently on the things that will produce your results, and to expect only the best to come from these efforts! But again, you must allow it!

Job eleven: instructional design consultant, University of South Florida

I was hired on at USF four months after I lost my job with Andersen Consulting. This career opportunity is responsible for my transition from my jobs to my dreams. This job was the catalyst for my concept of "Caught Between a Dream and a Job."

Lessons learned: transition, stability, creativity, teamwork, oneness, momentum, and the possibility of a dream job

What job/career taught you these skills?

_____

_____

My USF position was my dream job, and since I dedicate an entire chapter to that concept, I am not going to go into detail here. Just know that this opportunity is what helped me birth this entire concept, and it showed me very clearly why dreams are the greatest form of employment that exist today.

Now take a quick look back over the skills that you have acquired through the many jobs and careers that you have had. Every job was trying to teach you something—some skill, some ability, some character trait that will be imperative for you to demonstrate once you ultimately walk in your true destiny, calling, purpose, and dream.

Never look back on a job with negative conclusions, because even the worst of career decisions have taught you something necessary for success in your destiny. What have your jobs been preparing you for? When you look at the totality of your experiences, what flashing lights do you see indicating that you are now ready to take the steps necessary to walk in your dream? You have to know that even the job you have right now is preparing you to be a better CEO when you step out into the dream you feel in your heart.

CHAPTER SUMMARY

EIGHT POINTS TO PONDER DURING YOUR TRANSITION

1. Along our journey to success, we all have special people that help to develop and encourage us along the way. Never forget those people, and always love and celebrate them for the difference they make in your life.

2. You are a wonderful, unique, and powerful designer original. So design the life you want to live intentionally; don't default to the life you don't want accidentally.

3. Remember that the best way to predict the future is not to call a psychic or wait for a prophet to come to your church, but rather to create your future each day you wake up.

4. Understand that your life is one big white board that you get to decorate, design, and customize as you choose. Be resourceful, and make the most of this blessing called life.

5. Capitalize on the fact that you are a professional problem solver. Identify the gifts and talents you have, which we will do later in this book. Invest time in mastering those gifts to the best of your ability. Then, market your gift to the people and organizations that have the problem that your gifting solves!

6. Always outperform your paycheck. Remember what Zig Ziglar taught us. If we do more than we are paid to do, the day will come when we are paid more for what we do!

7. Look at every job or career position that you have ever had, including the one you have right now, as a teacher and a skill builder. No matter how big or small the job or career opportunity

was or is, let it teach you the skills you need to get you farther from the wage system and closer to the profit system.

8. Allow yourself to want what you really want, and then allow your best to come out of you on a daily basis.

CHAPTER 4

YOUR LIFE'S PURPOSE:
THE CATALYST TO YOUR DREAMS

The purpose of life is a life of purpose.[1]
—Robert Byrne

WARNING! THIS CHAPTER WILL MESS YOU UP—IN A VERY EMPOW-
ering and inspiring way. But know in advance that this chapter will
stretch you and challenge you because this chapter requires a great
deal of your own effort. In addition to reading, highlighting, understanding, and
applying—which is what you've been doing a great job of so far—this chapter
requires you to talk to and interact with me on a much more intimate and
personal level. Are you ready? OK then; let's go.

I am a fan of computer analogies and metaphors, so just like in chapter 3,
here is another one for you.

Let's say you buy a brand-new computer—a PC this time. You get it home
and open the box, plug in all the cables, and start working. All of a sudden, the
computer starts giving you error messages. Then you get a phone call from a
friend who wants to know if you are using certain features of the PC that are
really cool. You say no because you did not know that your computer could
do all that fancy stuff. You get off the phone and still see error messages, but
now you are even more curious about the many fancy features that your new
computer has that you have yet to take advantage of. What do you do?

Call the manufacturer or reach for the instruction manual, right? Right. But why? Because you know that the instruction manual is the manufacturer's mind put on paper. You know that if you call, you can get a friendly customer service associate to talk you through your issues. Notice what you did, my friend:

1. You realized that the issues you were dealing with were too advanced for your own resolution.

2. You realized that there was much more that you could do with your PC—if only you knew how.

3. You admitted that you did not have all the answers, so you consulted someone else.

4. The person that you consulted was the one who manufactured your product.

The point is very simple. Your life and your purpose in life are just like that new computer. There are certain issues that come up in life that you don't understand. And there are so many fancy things you can do with your life, especially when you design it, but it takes special consultation sessions to figure out how to work them all. Just as you would consult Microsoft (the manufacturer of Windows) if you wanted to know the purpose of certain applications, you must consult with the manufacturer and Creator of your life to truly understand your purpose.

Make no mistake about it; I am a man of faith. I believe that the Bible is the most powerful motivational book ever written. Therefore, in this chapter, don't be surprised to see a few major references to God.

Your life's purpose is your catalyst to your dreams. The ultimate goal that I want you to attain in reading and experiencing this book is to find that purpose so that you can make what you do full-time and for a living the thing that you love to do, the thing that you were put on this earth to do. You came to this earth for a reason. You are neither an accident nor a mistake. It does not matter how you got here. What matters is that you are here. Simply put, the people who live their purpose as their profession are the happiest, most prosperous, most balanced, impactful, influential, and giving people on the planet. And I want to help you become one of those people.

Purpose is the specific reason, intent, cause, explanation, or meaning for why a person, place, or thing exists. You were dropped on this earth with tremendous purpose. Nothing in life happens accidentally or without cause or reason behind it. All things happen for a reason. All the individuals you meet have purpose behind them. All the books you read have a purpose to serve in your life.

You are a blessed, uniquely special individual with tremendous gifts, talents, abilities, and skills that must be used to change and transform lives in some way. I believe that the moment you begin walking toward fulfilling your purpose in life, you transition from existing efficiently to living abundantly! You transition from a life by default to a life by divine design.

Most people are just out there existing—living from one day to the next, working from one day to the next, driving from one place to the next—with no real meaning behind why they do what they do. They are doing a good job at staying alive and paying the bills, but they are not living life with a true sense of significance. The goal of this life-changing chapter is to challenge you to discover and walk in the most powerful principle of life—purpose. My goal is also to show you how to connect that purpose to a profession that you can master, market, and get paid for!

POWERFUL POINTS ABOUT PURPOSE

1. Your purpose is permanent.

When you were dropped on this earth, God deposited within you an assignment—a mission, a reason for your existence. This world should be different before you die because you walked in your purpose. No matter who you are or what you do, you cannot shake your purpose. It's almost like your race and gender—you can't shake it. Well, nowadays with the advances in modern medicine and high-technology surgery you can, but you get my point. Your purpose is a part of you. It's the thing that gives your life direction and significance.

2. Your purpose is individual.

There is only one you. Therefore, your purpose is unique to you, your strengths, your weaknesses, your personality, and your life story. So you can stop spending precious time negatively comparing yourself to other people and being frustrated about the giftings that you did not get. If you needed someone else's gifting to accomplish your purpose, God would have blessed you with it. Therefore, if you don't have a particular gift, know that you don't need it to be successful or to walk in your purpose. Isn't that refreshing? In other words, if you can't sing worth a lick, don't be jealous of those who can. Just be confident in the fact that your purpose in life will not require that of you.

3. Your purpose births your gifts.

Your purpose is the womb that travailed all your gifts, talents, abilities, and skills. In other words, everything that you need in order to complete your assignment on Earth has already been given to you in the form of your natural personality, your skills, your makeup, and your divine design. There is a common thread amongst all your gifts, and that common thread is your purpose. Take me, for example. I speak, sing, write books and songs, coach people, consult with major companies and universities, produce CDs and DVDs, create training systems, and produce music as well. What is the common thread linking all of these things? Empowering communication that educates, equips, and motivates people and organizations to become all that they were designed to be. What about you? What is your mission/purpose? The tree illustration in the coming pages will help you further understand this point.

> A man who becomes conscious of the responsibility he bears toward a human being who affectionately waits for him, or to an unfinished work, will never be able to throw away his life. He knows the "why" for his existence, and is able to bear almost any "how."[2]
>
> —**Victor Frankl**

4. Your purpose solves a problem.

Every job, career, position, task, assignment, and purpose under the sky solves a problem that currently exists. A running back for a football team solves a position problem for a coach that needs more touchdowns. A faculty member at a college solves an instructional problem each day that they lecture. A sales clerk at a department store solves problems for new and existing customers. A car salesman solves a problem for someone with transportation needs. We all are gifted to solve problems for someone or something else. Your purpose, your assignment, solves a problem for somebody. I don't care if you flip hamburgers at a fast-food restaurant. Your culinary skill solves a hunger problem for a busy corporate CEO who needs a quick meal before attending a daylong board meeting. Look at your talents as problem solvers, and find someone out there who will pay you to solve problems for them.

5. Your purpose is multidimensional.

Your purpose and your assignment grow and expand as you move through different ages and stages of your life. When you are young, your primary purpose is to learn, grow, absorb, and develop into a self-sufficient person. As you get older, your purpose shifts from not only learning but also to teaching. Instead of being raised, you start to raise your own children. If you start a business, your purpose will expand to fit that. If you start a church, your purpose will expand to fit that. You get married, you have children, you buy a house; now you have a plethora of other assignments or purposes that your life serves. Being able to switch hats effectively is key once you really begin to walk in the multiplicities of your life's purpose.

6. Your purpose precedes your plans.

I am a believer, teacher, and student of goals. However, there are times when in spite of your goal or your plans, life will throw you a curveball for the sole purpose of moving you into your destiny much faster or more aggressively than you would have imagined. Remember, my plan was to work for a major corporation for at least ten years and then transition into full-time speaking. God had other plans. He knew that you would need this book, so He laid me off of my corporate job and transitioned me to a speaker, author, consultant, and life coach. That's why I am so glad that purpose precedes plans. Continue to plan your work and work your plan. But don't be surprised when purpose comes knocking at your door to transition you into a new season of your life.

7. Your purpose brings financial blessings.

Many times in life we are taught to expect our financial blessings to flow out of the reservoir of our educational accomplishments. These yield degrees of distinction—which we exchange for a career that we hope will sustain our families and ourselves. Well, while that may have been true in the past, and while that may be true for some still today, many people are finding out very quickly that the job market is not the greatest source of financial increase. My friend, I am a firm believer that when you really know your purpose in life and you master your purpose, people will pay you to do what you do. If you will invest the time necessary to begin to operate in your life's purpose and perform your purpose with quality and excellence, you will see financial prosperity like you have never known before.

Truths About Purpose

1. Everything begins and ends with purpose.

Wherever you are right now, take the time to notice everything around you: the chairs, tables, people, house, dishes, and carpet; cars and traffic; your office and the computers; the airport terminals and the luggage; the classroom and students; the grass and trees; the stores and the shoppers; couples and singles; waterfalls, fountains, sidewalks, and playgrounds. Everything that you can see and, more importantly, everything that you cannot see, began and will end with purpose. Everything that is something today started with a reason for its existence.

Think about the light bulb that is shining somewhere to illuminate the pages of this book so that you can read it. The purpose of that light bulb began in the mind of the inventor. The purpose of the light bulb ends when it burns out and is thrown away. It is thrown away because it has maximized its purpose and potential. Hence, it must be replaced.

Everything you do in this life should be done with a purpose. The friends you hang with should be chosen on purpose. The clothes you wear should be worn on purpose. The direction you drive to get to and from work should be chosen with purpose in mind. The places you go to eat, watch a movie, and shop should be purpose-driven. The house you build, the car you buy, the money you invest, the phone numbers that you store in your cell phone, the business cards you exchange—all of these things should be done with a overarching meaning, goal, reason, and intended outcome in mind because purpose brings clarity. You don't want to abuse any of these things in your life. Once you know the purpose for why you do what you do, you will do what you do better, for the right reasons, and then you expect the right results.

2. Contentment is found in the fulfillment of purpose.

I believe that true joy, significance, and satisfaction only come when we know within ourselves that we operate daily within the purpose for which God originally dropped us on this earth to do. You can earn millions of dollars performing a task well but never once walk in your purpose. You would have missed the entire mission (purpose) of your life. The goal of life is not for you to earn all the money, buy all the toys, eat all the food, suck up all the air, and drink of all the water you can. The true goal is for you to use everything that was deposited in you when you were dropped on this earth.

Ask Deion Sanders, who has said numerous times in interviews that he had millions of dollars in the bank (even a ten-thousand-dollar bed) but couldn't get any sleep. He had three hundred pairs of shoes but was not going anywhere in life. He had everything money could buy, but he lacked contentment. Then he discovered the one true thing that money can't buy—his divine purpose! Once he began walking in that, his life became full of contentment, joy, peace, and abundance. My friend, the real happiness that you seek in life is hidden behind the door of your purpose. Use this chapter to help you unlock that door and begin walking boldly in your life's assignment!

> Whatever is at the center of our life will be the source of our security, guidance, wisdom, and power.[4]
> —Stephen Covey

3. When purpose is unknown, abuse is inevitable.

I was a mischievous child, and many times I got in trouble because I messed with (and eventually broke) things that had great value to my parents. I mishandled those precious items because I did not understand or have knowledge of their purpose or significance. Because I was not aware of their value (purpose), I treated them as devalued objects of little importance—not intentionally but unknowingly. But trust me, after a few spankings, I learned the value of things very quickly.

The point of that short story is very powerful. We all have gifts, talents, abilities, and skills that have been given to us to help us facilitate our purpose, call, mission, and assignment in life. When the purpose or value of our life is unknown, we can abuse or mistreat our gifts and our life, trying to fit into society and trying to keep up with others. This is a detrimental mistake. Born priceless originals, many of us will die as cheap copies of someone else's purpose. We must stop the cookie-cutter approach to life and create our own destiny navigated by the steps toward fulfilling our life's purpose.

4. When purpose is known, greatness is guaranteed.

Once you know what you are called, assigned, destined, and equipped to do in this life, you are literally unstoppable. There are countless stories of people who discovered their purpose and in spite of lost family members, lost body parts, and lost senses, these people have amassed a level of success that is mind-boggling to say the least. Purpose is the master key to life. You can do everything else right, but if you did a great job at the wrong thing, the true mission still goes unaccomplished. However, if you do a good job at the right thing, the job gets done with the best level of quality that your life permitted.

5. Fulfillment of purpose requires support from others.

You, along with several billion other purpose-packed individuals, have been placed on this planet for a reason, for a mission. Part of your mission is to understand who you need on your team in order to accomplish the mission that you have been assigned. Always remember the words of a fellow speaker Tony McGee: "You have not been sent to earth on Mission Impossible. Rather, you have been placed here for Mission I'm Possible."[4] Whatever you truly see for yourself in your future, you can have. You must work smart and consistent, dedicated to fulfilling your life's purpose. But no man is an island. You can't do it alone, so stop trying, and receive the support of those God has blessed to be a help to you. Get the right people in your corner, and go after your dream as if your life depended on it—because it does! The goal of your life should be to live full and die completely empty. Give your everything because you can't take anything with you when you die.

You Must Be Like a Tree

A tree is symbolic of your life. Just like your life, a tree has five major components. Let's parallel the two and learn how we must be like a tree to truly walk in success on a daily basis.

1. Roots

The roots of a tree are symbolic of its foundation. These roots are the building blocks of the tree. They pull the nutrients, vitamins, and minerals from the soil to spread life throughout the tree. The only way to kill a tree is to cut it off from its roots. Without roots, a tree cannot live. In fact, when a tree begins to grow, it grows downward (roots) first, then suddenly it beings to sprout up to penetrate the soil. You are much the same. How well are you rooted and grounded? How strong is your root system to pull in the right nourishment? Look at the photo. Most trees' roots grow as broad as the branches on the tree.

2. Trunk

The trunk of a tree is symbolic of a solid mass of possibility. It represents your purpose. Every branch of a tree sprouts forth from the trunk. Its trunk determines a tree's height and width. Regardless of the season, the trunk of a tree stays the same, changing only for growth. The rings in the truck on the tree determine the age of a tree. It is one of the only aspects of a tree that maintains stability. Your trunk in life is your purpose and destiny. Your purpose, as you have learned in this chapter, is the one thing in your life that is permanent. It stabilizes and solidifies your reason for being on this earth. Your purpose is the fountain out of which everything else flows. What is your tree trunk in life? Not sure? Great! By the time you finish this chapter, you will know.

3. Branches

The branches of a tree are the extensions and expansions of the tree. Trees turn into fruit-producing agents as a result of the branches that grow from the trunk (purpose) of that tree. Your branches represent your gifts, talents, abilities, and skills. Your branches represent the innate talents that you were blessed with in order to bring your destiny to fruition. If the branches of a tree do not do their job of carrying nutrients from the trunk and roots to the fruit, the fruit will not be produced. Your natural gifts are the things that will produce ultimate fruit in your life. And you, my friend, are here on Earth to produce much fruit.

4. Fruit

Fruit is the final goal of the seed of a tree—not leaves but fruit. Fruit is the reason why the seed was planted in the first place. An end result—fruit (accomplishments)—is the reason why you are planted on this earth. You were built, designed, and engineered to produce results, goals, visions, dreams, families, communities, degrees, callings, books, CDs, contracts, winning teams, major corporations, businesses, Web sites, products, services, inventions, laws, policies, training programs, child-care programs, churches, scholarships, ministries, and the like. You were put here to produce something that would leave this world better than it was when you were born. What fruit have you produced?

The fruit that you have already produced is a good clue as to what your gifts are and, ultimately, the purpose for your life. A fruit tree tells on itself. You don't have to go up to an apple tree and ask the tree what type of tree it is. You can tell by looking at it what type of tree it is. Well, just as fruit trees tell on themselves, so do we. People can look at our lives and the accomplishments that we attained and determine what we are.

> Stop chasing the bling-
> bling, and focus on the
> main thing!
>
> —Delatorro L. McNeal II

5. Leaves

The leaves of a tree provide color and shade and make the tree breathtaking and wonderful to stare at. I like to call them the beautification of the tree. Those are the nice things about leaves. The bad thing about leaves is that they change colors, they fall off, and most of the time, they end up all over the yard— raked up and discarded. The pretty things of this life are much the same—cars, houses, clothes, home theater systems, jewelry, purses, iPods, gaming systems, and the like are all leaves. While nice and meaningful to a degree, these things are the most insignificant part of life. Ever notice how a strong storm or hurricane completely strips trees of their leaves? A major weather change can do it, too. Leaves come and go just like nice things. The storms of market downturns, layoffs, downsizing, stock market challenges, church splits, bad investments, crime, home invasions, and vandalism can easily blow the leaves of your nice things right to the ground.

Well, Del, that does not sound very motivational. Actually, it is. The point is that you should never spend the majority of your life trying to solely acquire the beautification of life. But rather, focus on producing the fruit that you were born to produce, and allow the pretty things of life to be by-products of your greatness.

You must be like a tree, rooted in the divine source that created you. The trunk of your purpose is the fountain out of which you allow your branches or gifts to flow. Once you extend your branches, take daily, consistent action steps to produce the fruit that you were planted to produce. As a reward of your production, the leaves (nice things) of life will automatically flow toward you.

WHAT TYPE OF PURPOSE PERSON ARE YOU?

Hang in there. You are getting closer to knowing what you have been put on Earth to do, and identification is the first step to making any major change in your life. You must identify where you are concerning your purpose. There are four categories that everyone falls into. The Purpose Inventory Test that I have included in this chapter will help you identify what category you fall in. Before you take the test, you must understand each of the purpose-type categories. After coaching, mentoring, counseling, interacting with, and interviewing thousands of people, these are the four categories that I have found most people fit into.

1. The unconsciously unpurposed

> He who knows not and knows that he knows not, but thinks that he knows!

These are people who don't know about the principle of purpose, and they are not doing anything to walk in their destiny. However, instead of seeking knowledge to bridge the intellectual gap, they act like they have themselves all together. Scripture reminds us that we perish because of a lack (lazy desire) of knowledge. This individual can be very dangerous and needs many walls and facades torn down before real change will manifest in his life.

2. The consciously unpurposed

> He who knows that he knows not!

These are people who are aware of the principle of purpose, but for either one of the following two reasons, they are not walking in it. First, they may have chosen to be rebellious to the call or plan of destiny on their lives. They could very well be running from it, as Simba did in *The Lion King*. Second, they could be aware of the principle but have no clue how to really discover their own unique purpose and begin to take steps to walk in it. I believe many people in our society are in this particular stage of purpose. There are many things that feed into this.

We live in an "I-want-to-be-like-Mike" society that says that it's cool and OK to want to be like someone else. And because we try so hard to be like other people, we focus externally instead of internally. In addition to that, we shun our own innate gifts in exchange for futile attempts to become "the next" someone else. It's like a cookie-cutter approach to life. Listen—don't live your life trying to be "the next" anybody. *Become the first you.* Become the one and only unique, special, blessed, gifted, and talented you. There is nothing wrong with admiring someone for their success. However, you should never live your life trying to become them. You will fail miserably. Not that you will fail in your efforts; you may actually do well. But you will ultimately end up failing yourself.

My dear friend and mentor Pastor Scott Thomas said in a sermon years ago, "Don't be easily impressed by people. Because if you can be easily impressed by people, you can be easily depressed by people." A person who can impress you and depress you simply by acting a certain way has way too much control over your emotions.

What you cannot produce, you will tend to imitate. This is powerful because when we become impressed with people, we start to focus on what they possess that we don't. This causes many people to want to dress, sound, walk, talk, and live like someone else. Every day you spend trying to copy someone else is a day you trade being a priceless original for being a cheap copy.

3. The unconsciously purposed

He who knows not that he knows!

These are people who by some happenstance in life have actually ended up stumbling into a career, job, position, or opportunity that is almost 100 percent in alignment with their ultimate purpose and destiny. They have no clue that they are doing what they are naturally and divinely gifted to do. So much so that it normally takes others to point it out for them. Usually these individuals enjoy what they do but don't believe they could make a living doing it. They do not realize that they possess a very rare and special gift that, if cultivated and marketed correctly, could bring them millions of dollars.

Many times this type of person manifests in the girl who designed her own prom dress because she has a natural flare for fashion, the gentleman who never goes to the barber because he cuts his own hair and everyone thinks he gets it done by a professional, or the person who details cars on weekends as a hobby, yet doesn't realize they can make a living at it.

One of the biggest and most accepted definitions of success is doing what you love to do and finding someone to pay you to do it. Think about it. If you needed to hire a maid to clean your house, would you hire someone who enjoys cleaning or would you hire the person who *loves* to clean? I'd choose the person who wakes up thinking of new ways to clean, daydreams about cleaning, and has a way of making things look nice.

People in this season of purpose remind me of the elephants, tigers, and other wild animals that you find in major zoos. Ever wonder why a two-hundred-pound tiger or a one-thousand-pound elephant can be controlled and directed by a ninety-pound animal trainer? Is it that the trainer is stronger? No way! The truth is that

He who knows and knows that he knows!

from birth the tiger and the elephant had been trained, shackled, and disciplined to obey the instructions of the trainer. Therefore, even when it's full grown and the animal's true potential far exceeds its present behavior, that elephant or tiger does not perform any differently because it does not know any better.

Imagine how awesome you really are. Imagine how bad to the bone you really are! Imagine how dangerous (in a positive way) you could be. Imagine the impact that you could make once you realize how blessed, gifted, powerful, and wonderfully you are made and how much destiny lies inside you.

4. The consciously purposed

These are people who know the power of walking in purpose and practice and experience that power daily because they are walking in it. Once you figure out and fully understand your purpose, baby, it's all over! Once you know and know that you know, you start to walk differently. You start to talk differently. Your life makes sense. Your battles and challenges even make sense because you know the gift that your challenges are coming against. Your victories are sweeter because you understand their significance in the grand scheme of things. Once you know and know that you know, you become *unstoppable*! Look out!

The leader within will begin to emerge, and the power behind your profession will be unleashed.

Purpose gives you access to your dreams. Would you try to use your car keys to get into your house? No, of course not! Because if you did, you would be using the car keys for the wrong purpose. Doing this too many times, and with too much force, could permanently damage the car keys to the point that they are no longer workable in your car. Well, just as you use the right keys for the right locks on doors, you must use your life for the right purpose so that you can unlock the blessings that lie behind the door of divine purpose in your life.

Discovering Your Life's Purpose Inventory

The questions that you are about to answer are 100 percent self-reflective. They will require you to really soul search, experience search, knowledge search, and any other kind of search you can think of.

You may not be able to answer some of these questions right away. Others, you will be able to whiz right through. This inventory of questions may be something you want to do alone. In fact, I recommend that your first pass-through be solo. The second time you go through it, get a best friend, spouse, or significant other involved because they will help you see things about yourself that you may be a little blind to.

The major goal is to try to get you to think systematically about the many aspects of your life and how those aspects relate to your ultimate purpose and destiny. Don't give up on this inventory. Don't allow yourself to get frustrated, annoyed, or irritated if you can't answer all the questions. This inventory is meant to get you excited and motivated by the fact that everything in your life has been shaping, designing, illustrating, and navigating you toward your purpose and destiny. By the time you finish this chapter you will have a road map for what direction you should be traveling in.

Remember the movie *Forrest Gump*? Do you remember the scene when he was playing football in college? Because he loved to just run, many times he would catch the ball and just start running. He had the ball and the opportunity, but he was simply running in the wrong direction. Well, my friend, you have won the race of life. You are here on Earth, and you have the ball (the blessing of life). Now, I want to show you how to run in the right direction so that you can score touchdowns in the end zone of your destiny all life long!

Repetition is the mother of skill. Play very close attention to your answers to each question. You will see the same answer come up several times during the inventory. This is a very good sign. This is exactly what should happen. This is confirmation that you are heading in the right direction. You will want to revisit this chapter several times before it all sinks in and you walk in all that is required of you. I am excited about the purpose-driven you that awaits you at the end of this chapter.

Purpose Inventory Test

Question Clusters

» Group One (1–5): Childhood Reflection

» Group Two (6–8): Life's Signals

» Group Three (9–17): People and Purpose

» Group Four (18–21): Creativity/Flow

» Group Five (22–25): Life, Death, and Legacy

» Group Six (26–28): Level Playing Fields

» Group Seven (29–30): Reflection and Action

Group One: Childhood Reflection

1. What do you love to do?

When you were designed, God placed inside of you a natural passion for specific things in life. There is a difference between what you like and what you love. The things that you love are the things you are passionate about. These are the things that you will put your whole heart into because your heart is where your passion and love lie. So in answering this question, focus on what you *really* love to do.

_____

_____

_____

2. When you were a child, what did you dream of becoming and why?
I am convinced that many of us would be much further in life if we had the same vision, imagination, and fearless attitude that we had as children. As adults we have become too educated about what we *can't* have. That's a bunch of garbage! Remember the art of allowing from the previous chapter. Here is where it comes into play. Allow yourself to really go back and envision who and what it is that you wanted to be when you were younger. I can truly say for myself that right now, I am living a large majority of what I wanted to be when I was younger. There are still a few things on my list to accomplish, but we are making great progress. However, I had to allow myself to really want that and be OK with wanting it.

_____

_____

_____

3. What are some of your favorite hobbies?
Your hobbies are the things that you enjoy and/or love doing in your spare time or in your leisure time. However, the reality is this: you can turn your play into your profit, your leisure into your labor, and your part-time hobby into your full-time profession once you discover and master the things that you love to do. As I said before, one of my favorite definitions for success is doing what you love to do and finding someone to pay you to do it!

_____

_____

_____

4. What are you naturally good at?
Do you realize that there is gold on the inside of you? Absolute, priceless, rare gold lies inside of you in the form of your gifts, talents, ideas, and skills. Never forget that, because the reality is that you will only pursue in life what you honestly feel you can apprehend. Know that you can

achieve untapped levels of greatness in your life. That's why God blessed you with the gifts.

_____

_____

_____

5. What do your close family and friends tell you that you are good at?
It's hard to see the picture when you are the frame. Sometimes we need someone on the outside looking in to tell us just how gifted we really are. Pay very close attention to the gifts that others celebrate within you. Family and friends are those who know you best, and they are encouraging your talent for a reason. Discover that thing, and use it.

_____

_____

_____

Group Two: Life's Signals

6. Looking back over your life, what are some instances that have been signaling you toward your destiny?
I believe that from the time you were born, life has been giving you certain clues and flashing lights as to what your true purpose is. For example, my mom says that when I was little, I would always say, "I can do it!" anytime she tried to help me with something. That same positive attitude I had back then has followed me to adulthood because I travel the world showing people that "they can do it"! What are some things that you used to say or do as a child that have carried over into your maturity now? These things are clues to point you in the right direction.

_____

_____

_____

7. When you find yourself bored with your current job/career, what do you dream about doing instead?

Many times our goals and dreams give us sneak previews of what is really to come in our lives. I can remember coming to tears while doing routine work in corporate America, because my destiny was flashing things upon my mind or heart. I had visions of me speaking to other corporations, colleges, churches, and associations. That vision is probably just as real for you now as it was for me then!

_____

_____

_____

8. What percentage of your true potential do you feel your present job demands of you, and how could you increase that number?

This is a powerful question! Most people's regular nine-to-five job only demands a small percentage of their true potential. And while many people find that very frustrating and upsetting, it is also very educational. Let's say that you're a lawyer, but while at work you're only using 20 percent of your true potential and gifts. What would you need to do at work to make that percentage increase? The answer to this question lets you know what you really should be focusing on. Remember, soar with your strengths!

_____

_____

_____

Group Three: People and Purpose

9. What were you doing when you made a major impact on someone else's life, and how did it make you feel?

The reality is that we all have a human need for significance. We all want and need to be significant in our own lives and in the lives of those around us. Your purpose will make a significant difference in someone else's life.

What have you done that has made significant positive differences in the lives of other people?

---

10. What were you doing when you were 100 percent at the top of your game?

We have all had those times in our lives when we were "in the zone." What were you doing when you felt a rush of energy and excitement, so much so that you felt "I was born to do this"? Find your zone, and work inside it daily. Learn to do what you love to do, and find someone to pay you to do it.

---

11. What is the common thread amongst all your gifts, talents, and abilities?

Amongst the many gifts and talents you have, there is one common thread. For example, I am a speaker, author, consultant, and success coach. I love to sing, write, and empower people. The common thread among them all is effective, empowering communication. What's yours?

---

12. What is the thing that people admire most about you?

The things that people admire about you are gifts that are natural to you. Pay close attention to what people are always complimenting you on and encouraging you to do. Even if it's something that you are a little embarrassed about, explore it. That just may be a key toward walking in your divine purpose.

_____

_____

_____

13. What gift do you have that negative people are jealous or envious of?

Hate, jealousy, and envy are excellent teachers. They inform you about what your powerful gifts are. If negative people talk about you because of your singing ability, chances are, you can probably sing very well! Whatever negative people say you shouldn't be doing is the very thing that positive people will challenge you to continue doing.

_____

_____

_____

14. What gift do you naturally possess that other people have to pay money to learn how to do?

This one is huge! Do you perform certain tasks so skillfully that the only way that others could compete with your gifting is through taking courses? You have certain skills that God just dropped on you. Other people are paying money and sitting in class to learn how to do what you do naturally. Be thankful right now for that, and use what you have. It's priceless!

_____

_____

_____

15. What problems in others are you good at solving?

I love this one, too. Begin to pay attention to the things that most people come to you for counsel about. What are the things that people are asking for your wisdom and input regarding? These are all telltale signs pointing directly toward your purpose. For example, if people are always coming to you asking for relationship advice, that's a really good sign that relationship counseling or coaching may be a target for you.

---

16. What talent do you execute so well that people cannot determine whether you are working or playing?

There is something that you do so well that if someone did not know you, they would be confused because they would not be able to tell if you were working hard or playing hard. For me, when I speak in front of a group, I am working and playing. I am having a blast doing what I love to do—while doing what I was designed to do. I confuse people who don't know me because I have so much fun living my dream. What is that for you?

---

17. What are some things that grieve or frustrate you the most about this life and society?

The problems that aggravate you the most in society are the things that you have been assigned to solve. Don't forget—your purpose solves a problem. My greatest frustration is people who live below their potential and privilege. I solve motivational challenges in people. What about you? Could it be the homeless, legislative policy, uneducated children, or abused women? The options are limitless, but your impact could last a lifetime.

Group Four: Creativity/Flow

18. When you watch movies and TV programs, what are the types of stories that impact you the most? Why?

The stories that move me the most are those about someone using their gift of speaking, writing, coaching, or counseling to speak a word of encouragement and empowerment to transform a person's life. The relationship between Mr. Miyagi and Daniel in *The Karate Kid* is a great example. Those types of movies and scenes move me to tears because that's exactly what I do. Well, what about you?

_____

_____

_____

19. If you could star in a blockbuster movie, what role would you play and why?

Sometimes we can't get a large vision for our own lives unless we envision it through the eyes of fantasy or movie magic. Most people have a favorite actor or actress who plays roles with a similar passion and conviction that we aim to guide our lives with. Having this understanding, if your life were a movie, what would be the major theme or storyline of it? Why would people want to come see it?

_____

_____

_____

20. What would you do with your life if you knew that you could not fail?

I once heard Les Brown, in one of his speeches, say, "Many people allow their fear of failure to outweigh their desire to succeed." I agree wholeheartedly. Failure is a natural part of the equation. You must fail;

it is required for success. My challenge to you is to feel the fear and do it anyhow!

_____

_____

_____

21. If an opportunity fairy really existed, what three wishes would you like granted?

The opportunities that you really want reveal the talents that you want to showcase. These talents will align with many of the gifts that you have already listed about yourself.

_____

_____

_____

Group Five: Life, Death, and Legacy

22. If you had three days to live, what would you do and why?

This is a critical question. This question really allows you to skip past the drama and focus on the things that mean the most to you and yours. The things that you would do in these three days represent the things that are most important, most pressing, most related to your legacy, and most related to your destiny. That's the focus!

_____

_____

_____

23. If you had ten minutes to address the world, what would you talk about and why?

Scripture reminds us that out of the abundance or overflow of our heart, the mouth speaks. If you had the world's ear, what would you say? What you would say is in direct relationship to the strongest passions and desires of your heart. This question forces you to focus on making a meaningful impact in the lives of people universally.

_____

_____

_____

24. At your funeral, what two sentences would you want people to be able to truthfully and sincerely speak of you?

In January 2003, my family went through a tremendous time because we lost two very special members of our family. In addition, our family's local church lost five members of their congregation within one month. Each weekend, we were attending funerals of key people within the church who all died unexpectedly. My friend, I ask you this question because at your funeral there should be certain positive things that everyone at your funeral says truthfully about you. Whatever they say is how your life will be summed up.

_____

_____

_____

25. What have you done to make this world different from the way you found it?

When you showed up on this earth, you were blessed with gifts that were installed into your life through your purpose so that you could change this world. Therefore, the things that you have done to make this world different are the things that are connected to your life's mission. You are here on a mission to rob the grave of its greatness and to change this world one person, one smile, one day, and one goal at a time.

_____

_____

_____

Group Six: Level Playing Field

26. If every job/career/calling in the world paid $15 per hour, what would you choose to do as a profession?

If money had no value or purpose, your desire to work for money would not exist. What would you do to be fulfilled every day?

_____

_____

_____

27. If you were laid off or fired tomorrow and your living expenses were covered for three months, how would you invest your time?

Many times we get stuck in the routine of making a living, and we forget to live our making! Well, if you no longer had the stress, pressure, and strain of making a living and you could design your day from start to finish—doing what you love instead of doing what "pays the bills"—what would your day look like?

_____

_____

_____

28. If you had one hundred thousand dollars cash today to start a business, what type of business would you start and why? Who would be your business partners?

Did you know that every ten seconds, a new home-based business is started somewhere in America? Well, now is your time to prepare for the type of business that you want, doing what you love to do, and finding consumers to pay you to do it. Turning your play into your profit is the ultimate goal here. It's possible! Who are the key players in your life right now who would be your business partners in the venture? Start working on this right now. Remember, you don't have to be great to get started, but you have to get started to be great!

_____

_____

_____

Group Seven: Reflection and Action

29. What are some common answers that continued to show up on your worksheet? What in this life is worth you procrastinating? Now is your time to walk in your purpose.

Now it's time for you to conduct a self-analysis of what the real answers to all your questions really mean. In order to do this, you need to start back from the beginning of this inventory and circle all of your common answers. The answers that continued to come up over and over again are flashing green lights to let you know that you have discovered a key component of your purpose and destiny in life. What came up for you? Check each box that applies.

❑ Writing

❑ Fitness training

❑ Speaking

❑ Counseling

❑ Advertising

❑ Selling

❑ Merchandising

❑ Wholesaling

❑ Constructing

❑ Landscaping

❑ Pastoring

❑ Teaching

❑ Training

❑ Photography

❑ Dancing

❑ Singing

❑ Operating

❑ Driving

❑ Banking

❑ Litigating

❑ Retailing

❑ Fashion designing

❑ Home building

❑ Preaching

❑ Real estate investing

❑ Mentoring

❑ Event planning

❑ Other _____

Next question: who in this world is worth putting your goals and dreams on hold? Let me help you—nobody! Nobody and nothing is worth you waiting another moment to go after your dream. You are here to make a tremendous difference. Don't allow the grave to rob you of your time each day with things like procrastination, the paralysis of analysis, fear, doubt, or distraction. Go for it!

30. What seven specific action steps can you implement right now that will allow you to begin walking in your divine purpose and passion in life?

I found that most people hide behind the excuse of task-complexity or a feeling of being overwhelmed as a way of getting out of taking action on their dreams. I want you to list (yes, physically write in this book right now) seven simple action steps that you can begin to take today that will allow you to start walking in alignment with your purpose and destiny in life. If you are already taking these steps, what can you do to take it to the next level? How can you penetrate the proverbial "glass ceiling"? What seven steps can you take right now? List them here, and begin each one with an action verb!

Here are a few examples:

» 1. Call a close friend, and tell them my goals/action steps so they can keep me accountable.

» 2. Meet with my mentor to have them sharpen my list.

» 3. Arise thirty minutes earlier each day and devote that time toward my own future.

» 4. Visit a professional in the area of my dream and ask them to help me.

» 5. Conduct online research about how to break into the field of my choice.

» 6. Complete this Purpose Inventory Test with someone I love and respect. Their opinion will empower me.

» 7. Read the next chapter of this book! (Smiles!)

Your turn.

» 1. _____

   _____

» 2 _____

   _____

» 3. _____

   _____

» 4. _____

   _____

» 5. _____

   _____

» 6. _____

   _____

» 7. _____

   _____

TWELVE THINGS YOU SHOULD DO—ON PURPOSE

1. Choose your associates and MMGs—on purpose.

Please, my friend, have a reason for why you surround yourself with the people that you do. Each person in your life either adds to your life or subtracts from it. They either multiply your efforts or they divide them. You have invested too much of yourself into your dream to allow *anyone* to delay your date with destiny. Choose your associates and your MMG (master mind group) intentionally. You should have a concrete reason for why each person you know and respect is in your life. Every person in your Master Mind Group should be pushing you, developing you, empowering you, stretching you toward greatness, financial excellence, and your destiny. Either you are developing them or they are developing you, but some type of development needs to be going on!

2. Network and meet new people—on purpose.

In his speeches, Zig Ziglar says, "Everyone is a prospect," which means that we must purposefully network and meet new individuals constantly. You can't get to greatness without other people. Positive people are your bridge to get you to the other side. Live your life based on the premise that you have not yet met 50 percent of the people who will be responsible for helping make your dream come true. Purposefully put yourself in the right place to meet the right people. Make it a goal to meet someone new each day. You never know whom that person may know. Remember, the people with whom you network ultimately determine your net worth.

3. Give and sow into others' lives—on purpose.

To whom much is given, much is required. In order to receive much, you must first give much. He who sows little will get little. But he who gives a lot gets a lot. Many millionaires are philanthropists are givers, tithers, and seed sowers. They invest in the visions and dreams of other people. We must do the same thing. Pour into someone else. How have I developed such strong relationships with key people of influence? I served them and invested in what they were doing, and in turn, I began to get what I needed.

4. Educate yourself on your topic—on purpose.

Dr. Mike Murdock says, "Pursuit is proof of passion."[5] I can tell how badly you want something not by how much you talk about it but by how much work you invest into it. You must educate yourself in your selected field of interest. You must know where the industry is headed and where your specific gifts fit into the big picture of the industry. You must research, join associations, attend conferences, and get weekly updates on the happenings with your industry. You will be amazed at how much knowledge there is out there. You can always learn more about your talents. This will keep you sharp and craving for continuous improvement.

5. Master your gifting—on purpose.

Sound similar to number four? Well, it might, but in truth they are very different. I know many people who read books, listen to tapes, and attend conferences, but they still never walk in their destiny. Their gift goes unmaximized because they do not put that knowledge into consistent practice. Let's take football for example. It's great to watch films of games, study playbooks, and research statistics, but nothing beats good old-fashioned practice. You must practice your talent regardless of how good you are. You must rehearse it and refine it, or you will be quickly outdated—then others will be getting the opportunities that could be yours.

6. Seek mentors and others you can mentor to develop you—on purpose.

You need someone who is more advanced than you in your life. You want to learn from them, glean from them, and be sharpened by their influence and wisdom. You need multiple mentors in different areas of your life—financial, spiritual, professional, and so on. Submit yourself to the advice, correction, and training of a mentor—someone who has been there and done that. Also find someone to pour your life lessons into. Find someone who wants to be where you are right now and potentially even further than you. Show them how to get where you are and how to learn from your mistakes so that they don't have to endure all of what you did. In other words, find someone who can help you cut your learning curve, and find someone whose learning curve you can cut.

7. Plan your life one year at a time, but live your life one day at a time—on purpose.

This is critical. I believe that we all have the power to create our destiny. What we do today literally shapes what we experience tomorrow. We don't have to dial 1-800 numbers to learn about what our future holds because the truth is that the future holds what you deposit into it today. If you invest nothing in tomorrow today, you will have nothing tomorrow. However, if you invest time today working on your dream, it will ripple into your tomorrow and bless your socks off. So plan your life for the year. You should know in January how you want December to close out. Once you have a vision for your year, wake up each morning and put your 100 percent best into that day, allowing it to get you a little closer to your yearlong goals.

8. Select your jobs and dreams—on purpose.

Pick jobs and careers that are in line with your purpose. Select each job not necessarily based on how much money you will earn, but on how closely it aligns with your destiny, knowing that it is only a stepping-stone to get you higher and closer to your manifestation of greatness. Know what your dream is. Have a clear picture of it in your mind and up on your walls.

9. Take consistent, daily action—on purpose.

Wake up each morning and envision a clean piece of paper (life) on which you have a few preprinted items, for example, traffic, school, work, getting dressed, eating, and so on. Now beyond the basics of day-to-day living, you have the creative power to add to your day certain consistent action steps that will get you much closer to your dream much faster. Decide that you are going to be a consistent person, and your life will change radically. Pick one or more action steps, and be like a stamp and stick to it until delivery is complete.

10. Share your gift with this world—on purpose.

Make up in your mind that the world needs the gift that you have. Why would you be placed on this earth if you were not meant to benefit this earth with your presence? Don't wait to be perfect—that will never happen. Don't wait for 100 percent support from everyone you know—that will never happen. Don't wait for all the money to be in the bank—that will never happen. Greatness is going to cost you. You will be required to take a step of faith. It will cost you believing enough in the dream that you will go after it with all you have in spite of the circumstances. Don't spend your life tuning your instrument; start making music now. Trust me, someone needs the gift that you have. Have you been rejected in spite of your best effort? Their loss! Pick up your pieces and move on.

11. Be thankful to the Creator for your purpose—on purpose.

Be thankful that God dropped each of us here for a unique, special, individual, and powerful reason. There is purpose behind every victory, failure, mountaintop, valley low, success, and storm. All the things that happen to us are trying to teach us something significant about life. So be thankful each day that your daily steps are aligned with a greater purpose and plan.

12. Play with the cards that you were issued—on purpose.

You were dealt a deck of playing cards called gifts, talents, abilities, and skills when you were dropped on this earth. Unfortunately, most of us don't play the game of life effectively because we are so focused on the cards that everyone else was dealt. Many people get jealous, envious, and hold grudges because of someone else's blessing. Well, my friend, we must understand that the more time we spend looking at someone else's cards, the less time we spend strategizing, planning, and preparing for our own success. Play with the cards that *you* were dealt. Stop feeling cheated or jipped in life. You have the best hand that was made for you. Use your cards, and play this game. And play to win!

DON'T LET IT DIE WITH YOU!

My friend, when this life is all over, everything that you did not give birth to (some form of documentation or communication of your dream or vision) will die with you. You must get your dream out because:

- When you die, it dies.
- When you die, that business idea dies.
- When you die, that book idea dies.
- When you die, that song lyric dies.

When you live your life, make sure that you are continually giving birth to something. Because even when you die, it lives! Think about it.

- When you die, it lives on.
- When you die, that business idea lives in your family.
- When you die, that song is sung and heard around the world.
- When you die, that dream was birthed and given life.

Sometimes our dreams will not come true within our lifetime, but as long as the dream and vision are put out there, then we all have something to live up to. Many believe that the great civil rights leader Dr. Martin Luther King Jr. died way before his time. Many believe that he died far before he ever saw the reward for his vision for equality brought to fruition. While that may be true, Dr. King's vision set the standard. His life and his commitment to the cause set the benchmark for a level of excellence that we all now must live up to. The purpose of his life was to raise the bar higher for national and international greatness. Now we live in a society that strives to attain the bar and surpass it. Goodness is free, but greatness will cost you. Are you willing to pay the price? Dr. King was!

CHAPTER SUMMARY

EIGHT POINTS TO PONDER DURING YOUR TRANSITION

1. You were strategically placed here on Earth for a special mission! You are no mistake, no accident, and no mishap. You are 100 percent destined for something special. No one was dropped on Earth with the exact same gifting that you possess.

2. The moment you start walking in your purpose is the moment you shift from existing efficiently to living abundantly. The abundant life you desire—financially, spiritually, professionally, and intellectually—is hidden behind the door of your purpose.

3. You are perfectly equipped for the assignment of your life. If you needed some other gifting, you would have been blessed with that, too. The absence of it is proof that you don't need it to be great.

4. True contentment is found in the fulfillment of your purpose, your mission, and your calling—not someone else's. You won't be comfortable in anything that's not your destiny.

5. Money is compensation for using your assignment to solve a problem. Do what you love to do, and you will find people who will pay you to do it!

6. Decide to be a consciously purposed individual—one who knows and knows that he knows. Be the type of person who connects their purpose to their profession.

7. Use the questions in this chapter to pull out of you everything that was deposited inside you, and allow the answers to steer you toward your divine purpose.

8. Do everything, every day, *on purpose*. Let the accidentals of life be gravy. Remember, it's the people who live their purpose while living their dreams who are the most fulfilled and content. Make that your story as well.

CHAPTER 5

THE ICEBERG THEORY: UTILIZING YOUR OCCUPATION TO EXPLODE YOUR POTENTIAL

What lies behind us and what lies before us are tiny
matters compared to what lies within us.[1]
—Ralph Waldo Emerson

ONGRATULATIONS ARE IN ORDER ONE MORE TIME! YOU'VE MADE IT TO the final chapter in the first section of this powerful and life-changing book. I celebrate you today for that. Now that we've gone in great detail to discover and uncover your purpose and how your life's purpose is connected to your calling and destiny, let's focus on how you can harness the power of your potential and use your occupation to become all that you were designed to be.

I love the beginning quotation by Ralph Waldo Emerson. It is one of my favorites because it is a consistent reminder that no matter what did or did not happen yesterday, and no matter how exciting or exhausting tomorrow may seem, neither of these two points and places in time can equate to the greatness that lies within us all as change agents in this world. Think about that. Yesterday is a powerful force because all of our memories and experiences are tied up in yesterday. Tomorrow is a powerful force because our hopes and dreams lie in tomorrow. But based on this quote, neither yesterday nor tomorrow holds a candle to the power that lies within us today. So what is it that lies on the inside of you, my friend? It's your potential! It's the part of you that always wants to grow, expand, move forward, evolve, improve, excel, surpass, rule, reign, achieve, get better, develop, and the like. The great thing about your potential is that it's yours, and it never stops leading you and challenging you toward your greatness. Purpose is the correct use of a thing, but potential is the maximum use of a thing. In other words, purpose, as we learned in the last chapter, is using your life for the right reason, and potential is using your life for all of its reasons. People of greatness—people like you and me—use our life's work to get all that is within us out of us and into this world so that we can fulfill the mission that Dr. Myles Munroe so eloquently stated.

Let me illustrate my point by asking you a question and having you participate in an activity with me.

WHAT DO YOU WANT YOUR TOMBSTONE TO SAY?

A speaker friend of mine from Nassau, Bahamas, said this one time: "Many people's tombstones will read: 'Here lies Jane Doe, who wished she woulda, shoulda, coulda...'"

And he is exactly right. Most people will die with their greatness still inside them, complaining to others about what they would have done, should have done, or could have done. Don't let that be your story. Now that you know that you have a "there" and now that you know your life's purpose and that you were meant to make a living by living your dream, you have to change what that tombstone will read.

> The purpose of potential is to empower us to live full and die empty.
>
> —Dr. Myles Munroe

Instead of saying, "Here lies Jim or Jane Doe, who wished they woulda, shoulda, coulda," replace it with, "Here lies Jim or Jane Doe, who has been there and done that!" Stephen Covey says that we have to begin with the end in mind, so let's create your epitaph right now!

Here is mine:

Here lies Delatorro L. McNeal II,
    who lived FULL and died COMPLETELY EMPTY!

Here lies Delatorro L. McNeal II,
    who has BEEN THERE and DONE THAT!

Man of God? Been there; done that!

Loving husband? Been there; done that!

Edifying father? Been there; done that!

Victorious son? Been there; done that!

Passionate brother? Been there; done that!

New York Times best-selling author? Been there; done that!

Life-changing speaker? Been there; done that!

Grammy Award–winning singer? Been there; done that!

College graduate? Been there; done that!

Philanthropist? Been there; done that!

Multimillionaire? Been there; done that!

Humble servant of mankind? Been there; done that!

Dream builder and goal maintainer? Been there; done that!

Legacy leaver? Been there; done that!

> **Questions provide the key to unlocking our unlimited potential.[2]**
> —**Anthony Robbins**

What about you? How will your tombstone read? Let's create it right now. I showed you mine; now it's your turn!

Here lies _____ who has lived _____

_____ and died _____.

Here lies _____ who has _____

_____ and _____.

1. _____ ? Been there; done that!

2. _____ ? Been there; done that!

3. _____ ? Been there; done that!

4. _____ ? Been there; done that!

5. _____ ? Been there; done that!

6. _____ ? Been there; done that!

7. _____ ? Been there; done that!

8. _____ ? Been there; done that!

9. _____ ? Been there; done that!

10. _____ ? Been there; done that!

You see, the bedrock of potential lies in your understanding that everything that exists, exists only because someone at some point in time decided to maximize their potential and get a thought, idea, concept, invention, novelty, product, service, good, commodity, trade, crop, recipe, book, theory, strategy, principle, vision, lesson, sermon, business, plan, goal, formula, or equation out of them. In other words, every day of our lives we live in houses that are nothing more than a brilliant collaboration of people's potential. We drive

> Potential is the
> outer working of the
> internal.
>
> —Author Unknown

cars that are mere expressions of someone's creative potential. We wear clothes that are simple, and sometimes complex, representations of the potential that came from the mind of a designer combined with the sewing skills of a seamstress.

In chapter 1, I told you that success is an inside-out job, and that has everything to do with potential. Oh, how I wish that potential was a physical part of our bodies. That way, we could see how much potential we had to work with. Then we could measure how much work we needed to put in to get the most potential out or how much encouragement to give someone else based on what we see as their amount of potential. But since we cannot see the potential hidden inside of us, the one thing we can know is that all of us were born with tons of it! Most of us just need to put in the work to get what's in us out!

EIGHT MISCONCEPTIONS ABOUT POTENTIAL

Over the last decade I have spent my life helping people from all walks of life maximize their potential. As I have done so, I have learned that there are a variety of misconceptions and/or misunderstandings that people have about potential. So let's invest a few moments of time to better understanding the gift of potential that we all were born with.

Misconception one: Potential is mainly for young people and children to develop.

One of the greatest mistakes that adults make is assuming that potential is something that only young people have and need to develop. For some reason, I find that many adults think that just because they have reached the age of parenthood, career success, and financial independence they have "arrived" and that potential is now something they must help young people with but stop developing for themselves. This is a dangerous and very limiting mind-set. Potential is important to develop at all ages and stages of life, not just in the beginning. A speaker friend of mine once said, "People are just like wheelbarrows; they only go as far as they are pushed." I believe that this is true. Yes, students and youth need to be pushed, but so do adults—businesspeople, entrepreneurs, you, me, your family, my family, your neighbors, my neighbors, politicians, millionaires, executives, teachers—everyone! We all need to continue to develop ourselves, because all of us, every last one of us, are under construction. No one is perfect, and no one has arrived. And a special footnote to parents: just because you have birthed children does not mean that you have birthed all of your potential. There is more inside of you—much more!

> **Never underestimate the power of dreams and the influence of the human spirit. We are all the same in this notion: The potential for greatness lives within each of us.[3]**
> **—Wilma Rudolph**

Misconception two: Potential can be outgrown; you can be too old for it.

Piggybacking on the first misconception, those who think they have arrived compound their ignorance by thinking that they are too old to become more of what they really wish they were. Many people stay in dead-end jobs and careers and don't take the step into entrepreneurship and business not because they don't have the skill, but rather because they think it's too late for them. They think that their boat has sailed, the plane has taken off, and that Elvis has left the building, so to speak. Garbage! It's all trash. You are never too old or too far in life to continue to strive for more and become better at this masterpiece called you. Just like my sixth grade teacher, Ms. Diane Williams, taught me, "The moment we were born into this world, our potential took off in front of us, and the whole race of life is about us catching up to ourselves." Your potential does not get tired, it does not take a rest, and it does not take a vacation just because you do. Your potential continues to run toward eternity, compelling you to be all you can be.

Always remember that your potential can always be maximized but never outgrown!

**Misconception three: Potential is just given to
certain people at birth.**

Once again, another limiting belief and excuse that comes from those who
have adopted the victim mentality in life. Some people, maybe even you at times,
may have thought that potential is only given to a specific group of people at birth.
Think about it. How convenient to think that your greatness was either given
to you in a big lump sum at birth or not at all.
Many people play the age card, the race card, the
gender card, the nationality card, and of course,
the money card to explain or justify why they can't
be successful, but it's all trash. Many people think
that those who were born into wealthy families
automatically have all the potential in the world,
and those born into poverty or limiting conditions
don't. This is error. The truth is, some of the most
successful people in our world—people whom I have already mentioned in this
book, people whom I have quoted, and people whom I have studied—have come
from nothing but saw something special in themselves that they wanted to share
with the world. Take Oprah Winfrey for example. She was not born into wealth.
She was not born a billionaire. She did not come out of the womb speaking as
eloquently and profoundly as she does today. However, she had the potential of a
billionaire communicator inside of her as a little girl in Mississippi, and she chose
to do something with that potential, and look at her today! It takes working your
potential out of you in order to see it work for you!

> No matter what the
> level of your ability,
> you have more
> potential than you
> can ever develop in a
> lifetime.[4]
>
> —James T. McCay

**Misconception four: Potential leaves you
if you make too many mistakes in life.**

I have coached and consulted with hundreds of people who believe that their
potential for success and happiness is over because they got divorced, had a child
out of wedlock, filed for bankruptcy, dropped out of college, got fired from their
job, went out of business, or any number of other reasons. Again, this is more
trash that needs to get set out on the curb of your consciousness to be picked
up and discarded. In fact, I would like to submit to you that it is the painful and
unfortunate situations and circumstances in life that act as the catalyst to explode
potential in people. It took Anthony Robbins being overweight and broke, living
in a run-down apartment for him to say enough is enough. He made a life and

paradigm shift, and look at the worldwide impact that he has made. Anthony Robbins is an internationally renowned peak performance expert, entrepreneur, and best-selling author. He has spoken to over three million people from eighty countries around the world. He decided to maximize his potential and dedicate his life to helping people from all around the world do the same. Your potential was assigned to you at birth and does not leave you to go hang out with someone else who is more interesting. Your potential is not flaky like people are. It's not impressed with the "bling-bling"; it simply cares about the main thing, and that is you! The comeback that you experience after your setback is what allows you to catch up, step-by-step, with your potential! Always be encouraged that your potential never leaves you. Even when you leave it to go do something stupid like we all have done at some point in our lives, your potential will still be there to encourage you to keep running your race.

Misconception five: Potential is only measured in terms of academics and economics.

In school we can easily measure potential by grades. If you are a B or C student, which most self-made millionaires in the United States were, then it is obvious that you have more potential because you are not currently making As. The same can be said for finances. Because both of these categories are calculated based on numbers and letters, it is easy to attach a value to them. However, potential in and of itself is far more than your income and GPA. In fact, Robert Kiyosaki proclaims in his book *Rich Dad, Poor Dad* that the most important number in your life after college is not your GPA but rather your credit score.[6] What happens for most people is that because we get so entrenched, programmed, and conditioned to potential being measured in numbers in the form of grades, we trade grades for financials once we

> The potential of the average person is like a huge ocean unsailed, a new continent unexplored, a world of possibilities waiting to be released and channeled toward some great good.[5]
> —Brian Tracy

become of age, and the new measurement of potential becomes who has the nicest cars, biggest bank accounts, the largest square footage homes, the most toys in the garage, the most expensive vacations, the biggest investment portfolios, and the most country club memberships. And while all of these various financial milestones and accoutrements are nice and valuable, none of them are a true reflection of the bedrock of one's potential. And so what most people do is they measure whether or not they have maximized their potential by how close they are to these financial milestones. They forget completely about measuring their potential for being a better parent, citizen, lover, spouse, sibling, mentor, volunteer, or leader in their community. These measurements of potential often take a backseat to academics and ultimately economics, which is unfortunate. The best thing is to live a life that empowers you and others while rewarding you financially and allowing all of your potential, not just two elements of it, to be maximized.

> The greatest crime in the world is not developing your potential. When you do what you do best, you are helping not only yourself but the world.
>
> —Roger Williams

Misconception six: Potential is the measurement of us against others.

Oftentimes when I talk with people about their potential—whether it be personal, professional, financial, marital, entrepreneurial, medical, emotional, or otherwise—they refer to where they are in life in direct comparison to where someone else is that they know. That other person is often their same age or in the same stage in life, and they feel like they have "one up" on life, simply because they are further along or better off than that one person or a few people they know.

Have you ever heard someone make statements like these?

- At least I am making better grades than...
- At least I am prettier or more handsome than...
- At least we don't have as much debt as...
- At least our children attend better schools than...
- At least I'm a better wife and mother than...
- At least my company has been featured in the paper more times than...
- At least our vacation was more elaborate than...
- At least we did not loose as much money in that investment as...
- At least our kids don't misbehave in public as badly as...

Each of these statements, and there are millions of them out there, are affirmations of potential based solely on a direct comparison between one person, situation, family, company, or what have you and another. Now, comparison and contrast are natural cognitive phenomena, and yes, they are necessary for us to discern, discriminate, and determine our preferences in life. However, negative comparisons for the purposes of defining potential should not be done.

You don't measure your own personal potential by how successful you are in comparison to someone else, because they don't have the same potential as you do. Just as your fingerprint is unique to you, along with your life's purpose, your potential is unique to you. Nobody has your exact potential. It's not that theirs is any less or any greater than yours; it's just different. And since it is different, you can't measure your success against someone else's and call that a maximized life. Your potential in any category is a personal, individual, and idiosyncratic measurement or you against yourself—no one and nothing else. For example, when I was in my twenties, and even still today, people would often tell me that I have accomplished much more than many people my own age. These people intend the statement to be a compliment, and I receive it as one, with a caveat. I always implore the person to understand that I never look at myself in that way because I don't measure my success with the measuring stick that belongs to someone else or society. I measure my success against where I am now versus where I see myself in my vision of the future.

> Everyone has inside himself a piece of good news! The good news is that you really don't know how great you can be, how much you can love, what you can accomplish, and what your potential is![6]
> —Anne Frank

Misconception seven: Potential is 100 percent up to God to maximize within us.

I could not wait to get to this one. I touched on this concept slightly in chapter 1, but now I would like to really drive this point home with absolute clarity. I believe that all human life and natural life came from God. I believe that God made mankind in His image and similitude. You also know by now that I believe that God put each of us here for a special purpose and jam-packed us with limitless potential to do, be, and have anything we would like to do, be, and have. I believe that with God's help, human beings can accomplish anything.

However, I also and ultimately believe that God gives us resources, and it is up to us to utilize those resources to the fullest to get the maximum out of our lives and life experiences. I know so many people who feel that if it is God's will for them to be a successful and fully maximized person that God would just magically do it all for them while they just sit back and bless His holy name. And

> There is no man living who isn't capable of doing more than he thinks he can do.[8]
>
> —Henry Ford

in my opinion, this could not be further from the truth. I believe that God dropped each of us here to impact this world for the better, and it is our job to take all of our divinely inspired resources such as our personality, knowledge, skills, abilities, talents, ideas, giftings, purpose, passion, determination, resiliency, fortitude, tenacity, relationships, family, community, wisdom, education, information, technology, and innovation to achieve our goals and dreams. I believe that the assumption "If success is going to happen, God is going to do it all" completely destroys personal motivation to achieve on your own. The limitless potential in your life was God's gift to you. The maximization and ultimate utilization of that potential through your life is your gift back to God. Play your part.

Misconception eight: Potential comes out automatically!

I have never met an ASP before—an accidentally successful person! Everyone whom I have ever met, studied, researched, or connected with have all been intentional about getting their potential out of them and into this world. Potential does not just come out of a person by mistake, happenstance, a whim, or without unction. Potential is not maximized just because you get older or because you become smarter. As we have already learned, knowledge alone is not power! Life experiences have a way of drawing the potential out of us however we allow that potential to come out. You see, many people suppress their potential. They keep a lid on it because, after all, that is easier than trying and failing at something. They take the mind-set that says, "Whatever is in me will eventually come out on its own without my effort." This type of stinkin' thinkin' keeps most people singing their shoulda-coulda-wouldas all the way into old age. The only way that potential comes out automatically is once you have conditioned yourself to win and succeed through right actions, thoughts, habits, and relationships! Once these four things are in place and working together consistently, then your potential begins to emerge automatically.

There is no such thing as an overnight success! Many people, stars, celebrities, artists, and people whom we see in the limelight that we call overnight successes are people who began their journey to success many years ago. It's just that we did not know about those people back then because they did not have any media coverage. Many of them developed their gifts and talents on the backside of the desert and revealed themselves once their gifting was at a level where once exposed would generate much hype. Success takes work—hard work and smart work.

> I can't believe that
> God put us on this
> earth to be ordinary.
> —Lou Holtz

POTENTIAL BOILED DOWN

Now that the misconceptions have been identified and remedied, what we should know by now about potential is that we all have it and that basically it is a measurement of a gap that exists between where we are presently and where we wish to be in the future. So with that said, allow me to ask you a few questions. Answer them by simply circling your response.

1. Can you be a better citizen of your country and a more productive human being?

   Yes or No

2. Can you be a better spouse or significant other in some way, shape, or form?

   Yes or No

3. Can you be a better son or daughter and share more of yourself with your family?

   Yes or No

4. Can you impact more lives with the gifts and talents that are inside of you?

   Yes or No

5. Can you feel and express more love than you've felt and expressed before?

   Yes or No

6. Can you earn more money and more respect than you have earned to date?

Yes or No

7. Can you be a better student in school, college, or in life than you've been before?

Yes or No

8. Can you be a better leader, example, mentor, and role model than you've been?

Yes or No

9. Can you be a better reflection of God's love for others through your lifestyle?

Yes or No

10. Can you grow in knowledge, wisdom, and understanding beyond where you are?

Yes or No

11. Could you earn more and create more if you were your own boss?

Yes or No

12. Could you enjoy more vacations, less stress, and more joy and contentment in life?

Yes or No

My friend, I could ask you hundreds of questions just like these, but I am sure that your answers would probably consistently match mine. All yeses! You see, I truly believe that we all have room to grow in life. We all have the ability for more, and that's potential. It's the affirmation of a possibility! Potential is admitting to the fact that, yes, it is possible that there could be better in my life if I just chose to manifest it. What a tragedy to live your life and not become the person that you know deep down inside you were meant to be! That's why I am so glad that you are experiencing and applying this book to your

> The only place success comes before work is the dictionary.
>
> —Author Unknown

life. Writing this book is an expression of my potential, just as reading it for you is an expression of yours.

LIMITED FUNCTIONALITY

I have a MacBook Pro laptop computer by Apple. I absolutely love it! I am ten times more productive on this device then I was on my PC laptops of the past, because I can do so much more on it. I can write books, type letters, take photos, capture video footage, create DVDs, make and duplicate CDs, research online, check and respond to e-mail, shop the Internet, book business and personal vacations, graphically design business cards, manipulate photos and images, create slideshows, conduct video conferences via iChat, build and present PowerPoint presentations, purchase and download music, play movies, produce music, create audio books, and tons more. Now, with all of that said, let me ask you a question. Imagine someone gave me this same laptop a year ago instead of me having to purchase it myself. If once I got it, I only utilized it to check e-mail, would I be maximizing the potential of that laptop? No, not at all. Although I would be using the laptop for the correct purpose, or one of its purposes, I would not be maximizing the potential, the capacity, the largesse, or the fullness of it by a long shot.

> The greatest waste in the world is the undeveloped difference between what we are and what we could become.
> —Ben Herbster

I find that most people treat their life just like that laptop. The laptop, which was built to function at full capacity and perform tens of thousands of functions, goes drastically underutilized because the owner only wants to check e-mail.

Many of us go through life on what I like to call "limited functionality." We do the same thing day in and day out, week in and week out—work, school, home, gym, couch, TV, church, and so on—and we use our limitless life for a few routine and limited daily functions, then we shut it down. What a waste! Life is meant to be explored, experienced, enjoyed, fulfilled, and rewarding! Make a personal, professional, spiritual, emotional, relational, educational, financial, psychological, and physical commitment to yourself right here and right now that you are NOT going to let all the cool and exciting features, facets, and functions of your limitless life go unmaximized! Make a decision that you are going to play full out in this life. After all, this life is not a rehearsal. It's short like a vapor—here today and gone tomorrow. So while we have the greatest gift we can ever have—the present—why not seize it and live it to the fullest? There is so much you can do with your life!

My poster child for potential is a guy by the name of Simba. I am sure you remember Simba from Disney's *The Lion King*. Simba's father, Mufasa, was the king of Pride Rock. Simba was a very excited and anxious young cub who wanted nothing more than to be king like his dad and follow in his father's footsteps. Now, the interesting thing is that Simba could not wait to be king, but in reality he could not wait to be . . . what he already was! Think about it. Did Simba have to do anything or fill out any applications or interview somewhere to apply to be the king? No. Simba was already born into that purpose and born with king potential as his birthright! All Simba had to do was learn from his father, keep his nose clean, and when the sun set on Mufasa's time as king, it would imme-diately rise on Simba's time. The amazing reality that I learned from watching this movie more than thirty times is one that is very critical to this chapter. You see, my friend, you already are the person you want to become. It's just that the person you want to become is in seed form! Simba didn't realize that he already was the king, but he was a little king or a king in training.

This point is so very powerful that I need to stop to make sure you caught it. What I am trying to tell you is that whoever or whatever it is you want to be, you already are that thing or that person; it's just in baby stage. In other words:

- You already are the CEO of your own company.

- You already are the captain of your destiny.

- You already are in control of your financial future.

- You already are a successful entrepreneur with global products and services.

- You already are a stay-at-home mom and businesswoman all rolled into one.

- You already have the financial capital to start your business venture.

- You already have the creative ideas and witty inventions necessary to develop a brand.

- You've already transitioned from job living into dream living.

- You already are what you are trying to become; it's just in Simba form right now.

That should be extremely empowering to you, my friend! It is to me, because although you may think that I have arrived at my "there" and that I am already where I want to be, please know that I am still under construction, and the fullness of who Delatorro L. McNeal II is, is still evolving out of me on a daily basis. I have to constantly remind myself that I already am the person that I am continually striving to become, just as you are already the person that you are striving to become.

Now, back to Simba. Because he did not realize how great he already was, instead of acting like a little king, he acted more like a big kid, so much so that his behavior got him into a lot of trouble that his father had to consistently bail him out of—until one day when his father was killed by Simba's Uncle Scar. Once that happened, Simba automatically became king. However, since it happened so fast and unexpectedly, Simba ran from his responsibility to go hang out with his friends Timon and Pumbaa instead of stepping proudly into his purpose and potential as king. You see, life presents us with two options: (1) we can either proactively develop our potential in preparation to the opportunities we expect in our future, or (2) we can reactively develop our potential in response to tough situations that life hands us. I always try to be proactive about developing myself so that life does not have to force me to develop on the rebound. Truth is, you never know when it will be your time to shine, your time to produce, and your time to be in the spotlight. So it is always best to be prepared! Commit yourself to the process of development. Simba's problem was that he did not do this. Instead, he ran from his problems, ignored them as if they did not exist, and did what was comfortable rather than what was necessary. I can say that I have done this before as well. Have you? Had he stayed and surrounded himself with his family and friends that wanted to see him mature into king, he would have developed much faster.

> What you can become you are already.
> —Hebbel Friedrich

Since you already are what you want to become in seed form, why not decide today that you will operate from a new paradigm, one that says you will conduct yourself as if you already are what you want to be. So if you want to be a millionaire entrepreneur one day, start conducting yourself like people who are millionaire entrepreneurs. Do what they do, and you will become what they are! It's that simple.

FORMS OF POTENTIAL

Just as there are many different types of potential, most of which we have already mentioned in this chapter, there are also many forms of potential. So let's examine four forms of potential so that you will be able to recognize potential when you see it in yourself, in others, in opportunities, in relationships, and in organizations. Potential often takes the form of one of these four components.

1. Untapped resources

Many times people don't maximize their potential because they don't take full advantage of all the resources that are around them. And when we think of the word *resources*, many things should come to our minds. Think about it for a second; there are tons of resources at our disposal all the time that we often don't work to the max.

- Human resources
- Material resources
- Technological resources
- Emotional resources
- Natural resources
- Financial resources
- Relational resources
- Spiritual resources
- Chronological resources
- Intellectual resources

The manifestation of this untapped potential comes in the form of people you have not met or people you have met but have not maximized your connection with yet. These could be business cards that you collected and have not followed up on. These could be sales leads that have gone uncontacted. These could be resources of financial or intellectual capital that you have not discovered or really chosen to uncover due to laziness, being understaffed, or just procrastination. Potential is everywhere!

It's not a tragedy to be prepared without an opportunity, but it is a tragedy to have an opportunity and not be prepared![9]

—Les Brown

Dr. Mike Murdock has written hundreds of books, but he has one that I really love and highly recommend. It's called *The Law of Recognition*. In this book, he says that everything we want and need in life is already in our life in some way or another. It's just a problem of recognition. As soon as we recognize who or what it is, and that they or it exists to benefit us, the light goes on, and we see an opportunity to seize that moment.

> **You are more than what you have become.**
>
> —**Mufasa,**
> *The Lion King*

What resources in your life have gone untapped? Are there things you can do to bring awareness to the potential of resources that already exist in your life? Is it possible that your soul mate is someone whom you've already met, but you just have not looked at them in that special way before? Is it possible that some of the things you wish, dream, and pray for already exist in your life, but they have not been tapped into?

2. Dormant abilities

This is a big one. I have been very guilty of this in my past, especially when I was younger. In truth, I believe we all have been guilty of this one. People with dormant abilities can sing, but they don't. They can write, but they won't. They can dance, they can produce, they can design, they can build, they can engineer, they can sell, they can administrate, they can account, they can develop, they can teach, they can motivate...but they just don't! Their abilities lie dormant inside of them. These people are often jealous and critical of others who are expressing their talents, being overly judgmental toward someone who has successfully taken steps toward greatness that they themselves have not taken. Sound familiar? There is absolute *gold* on the inside of every person; it just needs to be extracted!

I am a firm believer that sometimes we don't pick the books we read; they pick us. Many times at our jobs, careers, and callings, we don't complete the work—the work is completing us. Why? Because many times life hands us different circumstances, tests, and assessments to work the potential, the ability, and the talents out of us. Many people don't discover how physically strong they are until they get in a battle. Most of us don't understand how resilient our human spirit is until we have to bounce back from a major setback in life. You have a choice—either you can be hard on yourself, or life will do it for you. Either way, your abilities will be worked out of you—believe that. Simba had to learn this lesson. He ran from his potential and purpose so long that it took his father coming back to him in a dream to let him know that he was made for more than what he was displaying.

Mufasa was speaking to the dormant abilities that he knew his son, Simba, had but just was not exhibiting. After that dream, Rafiki the monkey helped pull the greatness out of Simba, and of course, you know how the story ends. If not, go rent or purchase the movie.

Why is it that the recording artist Prince can play more than seven different instruments, while some people like myself can't play one really well? It's because Prince invested the time in getting those dormant abilities out of him, and I chose to invest my time in different areas. That phrase is very interesting— *dormant abilities*. Many volcanoes lie dormant for years and years, but one day they decide to erupt, and once they do, everyone and everything around them better look out, because hot lava is coming. And I believe that many people lie dormant, working jobs to pay bills rather than working dreams to pay their destiny. But I hope that this book will challenge you to begin to erupt and positively explode your gifts and talents on everything in your path!

3. Unused power

I believe we all have power within us—power we don't often realize.

- Power to focus
- Power to dream
- Power to love
- Power to create
- Power to invest
- Power to change
- Power to inspire
- Power to motivate
- Power to follow God
- Power to forgive
- Power to serve
- Power to work
- Power to learn
- Power to apply what we learn

- Power to concentrate
- Power to make a comeback
- Power to attract anything
- Power to graduate
- Power to excel
- Power to live abundantly

Now, all this power is great, but only if it is used! Most of us don't use our power. We let life just act on us, making us *reactive*, instead of us acting on life, making us *proactive*. Let me ask you a question. Would you go to the store and buy batteries for a major device you had at home, only to get home and put the batteries away in a drawer somewhere never to be used? You probably would not. Instead, you would come home and immediately install the batteries into the device and continue enjoying that device, toy, tool, or appliance. However, if you did come home and store the batteries rather than use them, you could not complain about your life not being complete without the use of that device. Why? Because you failed to use the power you possessed through the purchase of the batteries.

As you learned earlier in this book, I worked for a consulting firm in my early twenties. I did a lot of organizational development projects for major utility clients. Well, during my stint on some of those projects, I learned some really awesome things about power. I learned that electrical power cannot be stored or contained. I learned that as soon as electrical power is created, it has to immediately be transmitted and distributed throughout the power lines. Wow! Now, let's look at this from the human perspective. Our power to do all the things I listed previously cannot be stored or contained. It must be transmitted. So we must begin to transmit our creative power into action steps that will turn cognition into creation, thinking into trying, dreaming into doing, and wanting into walking. My friend, there is too much power within you! You think that Superman, Spiderman, Wonder Woman, the Fantastic Four, or the Transformers have power? Their power pales in comparison to the power that you have within to be whoever you chose to be!

4. Unfulfilled purpose

Have you ever known someone who was walking in their life's purpose, but they were not maximizing the potential of that gifting in their life? I am sure you know of someone like that. They may be closer than you think. (Smiles!)

You see, I believe that in order to really be great, we must maximize the potential of our purpose.

Let's take teaching as an example. If teaching is your purpose and you are teaching now, that is great. However, are there others whom you could teach? Are there additional subjects or topics you could teach? Are there new types of students you could teach? Are there new methodologies that you could apply in your classroom? Could you change your classroom? Make it outdoors? Take more field trips to really create an illustrated message of the learning? Could you teach in more formats than the norm? What about teaching through books, seminars, keynotes, webinars, panel discussions, chat rooms, private parties, and one-on-one/group coaching? There are so many ways to teach besides just lecturing in front of the same group of students on a daily basis.

These are just a few examples of how we (regardless of our industry) can maximize the potential of our purpose and thus leave a lasting impression on the hearts and minds of those we serve.

One final thought on this topic before we move on. I believe that you and I must not look at potential as optional. It is mandatory that your potential excites you, motivates you, and compels you to maximize it. The gap between where you are and where you want to be should not be something that makes you comfortable. You should be a little irritated by it. This healthy irritation will be exactly what you need to continue to get up early in the morning and invest time later in the evening.

> When we treat man as he is, we make him worse than he is; when we treat him as if he already were what he potentially could be, we make him what he should be.[11]
>
> —Johann Wolfgang von Goethe

I like the way my speaker friend Gary Coxe talks about it in terms of when entrepreneurs first start a business. He says, "In the beginnings of a business, you will have more time than money to invest. So invest it like a madman. Soon you will experience a reversal, where you will have more money than time—that's when you hire someone to complete some of your tasks for you because you need to invest your potential in other places."[10]

Be mindful of these various forms of potential: untapped resources, dormant abilities, unused power, and unfulfilled purpose. Each of these and many others can be the cause of major success in your life or major failure. The choice is yours. Decide today to maximize your potential so that you can live full and die empty.

THE ICEBERG THEORY

Take a good hard look at this image, because in reality you are looking in the mirror!

In order to maximize our true potential, we must understand that we all are like icebergs. Humans have different shapes, heights, sizes, colors, depths of knowledge and understanding, drifting speeds (traveling through life at different accelerations), and ultimate destinations. Our lives mirror the major characteristics of an iceberg.

- Insight about icebergs: All icebergs are derived from much larger masses than themselves.

- Insight about you: You were derived from a source much greater than yourself—God!

- Insight about icebergs: Icebergs are very unstable without a solid foundation.

- Insight about you: Without a solid foundation, you can be a very unstable human being. Remember the tree illustration? Without a solid root system as the foundation, the tree can't live.

- Insight about icebergs: All icebergs tower above the water level to some degree or another.

- Insight about you: You are a success! You stand out in your own unique, individual, special, and destined way.

- Insight about icebergs: Seventy to 90 percent of an iceberg's true mass is hidden below the waterline.

- Insight about you: Seventy to 90 percent of who you really are is yet to be seen. It's hidden below the waterline of your potential.

ENEMIES OF YOUR POTENTIAL

As we begin to bring this chapter and the first half of this book to a close, allow me to remind you of a few enemies and allies to your greatness. Understanding the things that will empower you to succeed versus those things designed to make you fail will be vital to your ability to leave the nine-to-five job behind and step into the life you've always dreamed of.

Following are a few enemies to your potential:

1. Thinking small

Everything begins with your mind-set. If you want big results, you have to think big thoughts. It takes the same brainwaves to process a small thought as it does a big one, so why not think big and believe for the best that life has to offer?

2. Staying where you are occupationally

If you purchased this book or someone gave it to you and you have read this far, you are obviously not satisfied with your current occupation. You want

> It's not what you've got, it's what you use that makes a difference.[12]
>
> —Zig Ziglar

change, and I am proud of you for that. But please understand that staying where you are is indeed an enemy to your greatness. You have to transition out of that place and into the place that you desire, and the second half of this book is going to tell you exactly how to do that.

3. Trying to figure out the how

This is a biggie! So many people abort the "there" in their lives because they cannot figure out the "how." They think that in order to get "there," the entire "how" has to be 100 percent clear from the outset, and that almost never happens. Many of the most successful people in our world today had not a clue how they were going to do what they have done. They just knew enough and believed enough to keep taking the next step. Don't live in the how; live in the now and let the details fall into place naturally.

4. Associating with negative people

This will be a very short one, because it's self-explanatory. Eliminate negative people—family, friends, business colleagues, roommates, neighbors, and whoever else—from your inner and outer circle. Delete them from your cell phone, black book, Rolodex, electronic address book, and all other forms of organization. Don't tell negative people about *any* aspect of your transition. In fact, don't even tell negative people that you are reading this book right now! Run from negative people!

> The only thing worse than being born blind is living with sight but no vision!
> —Helen Keller

5. Enjoying your current success too long

It is very important that you reward yourself when you succeed at something. It is also important that once you succeed, you take a rest and recover from what you have accomplished. However, once you have done these things, make sure that you keep climbing. Sometimes today's success can be the enemy to tomorrow's achievement. Living in the memories of yesterday's trophies can keep you from seeing today's finish line.

6. Being an information junkie

Most people are information junkies rather than application addicts! They go from workshop to workshop, conference to conference, seminar to seminar, service to service, and book to book acquiring a lot of information, but not experiencing real transformation because there was not an application of their knowledge. I would much rather go to one conference and apply 90 percent of what I learned than go to nine conferences and only apply 5 percent of what I learned. Being a junkie for just information alone will limit your potential. It's only those who become application addicts who really seize their greatness.

7. Living without vision

You have to see it to manifest it. That's why I asked you to look in the mirror at the photo of the iceberg, because you have to envision how much more there really is to you as an individual. Have you ever looked at your boss and said to yourself, "This person has no clue who I really am, how powerful I really am, or how valuable I really am?" I am sure you have! Your problem with your boss was that your boss did not have a large enough vision of you. Well, in order for others to have a larger vision of you, you have to have a larger vision of yourself. I will talk much more about this in the second half of the book, but simply put, you have to visualize it so you can materialize it.

> Leadership is unlocking people's potential to become better.[13]
>
> —**Bill Bradley**

FRIENDS OF YOUR POTENTIAL

OK, so we now know that your potential has some enemies. Great. Let's take a quick look at some friends that your potential has. Since the second half of this book goes into great detail on each of these, I am only going to list them for you now so you can have a sneak preview of what's to come. The point remains, however, that for every foe to your potential there are at least two friends to that same potential. Choose now to gravitate toward the friends of your future and not the foes. The following list of things will explode *all* types and forms of your potential in this lifetime like nothing else will.

- Right relationships
- Seminars and conferences
- Speakers, authors, and teachers
- Prayer and meditation
- Opportunities
- Giving and contribution
- Exposure
- Vision
- Faith
- Leadership
- Persistence
- Good books, DVDs, and CDs
- Coaches, trainers, and mentors
- Experts and preachers
- Callings and dreams
- Experience
- Service
- Goals
- Action
- Determination
- Failure
- Environment

CHAPTER SUMMARY

EIGHT POINTS TO PONDER
DURING YOUR TRANSITION

1. Walking in your life's purpose and maximizing your life's potential are two separate issues. Purpose is the correct use of your life. Potential is the maximum use of your life.

2. Remember that the bedrock of potential lies in your understanding that everything that exists, exists only because someone at some point in time decided to maximize their potential.

3. Realize that potential is important to develop at all ages and stages of life, not just in the beginning. Additionally, keep in mind that all of us, no matter how successful or unsuccessful, are still under construction.

4. Always know that your potential never gives up on you or leaves you because you make mistakes or experience misfortune in life. In fact, your potential can use those failures and grow stronger because of them if your attitude is right! Also remember that your potential was assigned to you at birth and does not leave you to go hang out with someone else who is more interesting.

5. Know that life was meant to be abundant and exciting! Realize that your potential is absolutely limitless and that there is nothing above you preventing you from climbing higher. Although others may slow you down temporarily, only you can stop yourself permanently. Don't live life on limited functionality, because you are unlimited!

6. Remember that the forms of potential come in untapped resources, dormant abilities, unused power, and unfulfilled purpose. Each of

these forms is simply awaiting your intelligent action to transform from possibilities to realities in your life.

7. When you see that iceberg, think of yourself, and remind yourself that 70 to 90 percent of your greatness is still to be seen and experienced. Don't cheat this world out of enjoying your potential. Know that your ultimate occupational fulfillment only comes when you are in the place where your potential is maximized.

8. Remember that although you have several enemies of your potential, the friends of your potential are far greater! Stop trying to figure out the how, and live in the *now*! Keep the right attitude, people, and resources around your potential, and watch it grow and explode from you like hot lava!

Section 2

Hiring Yourself
and Landing Your
Real Dream Job

CHAPTER 6

IT'S TIME TO TRANSITION

The only thing that stands between a man and what he
wants from life is often merely the will to try it and the
faith to believe that it is possible.[1]
—David Viscott

WELCOME TO THE SECOND HALF OF *CAUGHT BETWEEN A DREAM AND a Job*! I am very proud that you have made it this far in the book, so much so that I would like you to do something for me. As is customary with many of my books, I would like you to take a moment and e-mail me at Caught@DelMcneal.com and let me know what this book has meant to you so far. Just for writing me, my staff will send you a free article and audio message from me to you, directly in your e-mail box. Deal? Cool.

Now that we are in the second half of the book, allow me to quickly prepare you for the major differences that you will encounter in this section. The first half of this book was designed to be more conceptual, intellectual, psychological, and internally rewarding and empowering. The second half, starting with this section and this chapter, is designed to be practical, tangible, instructional, strategic, action oriented, and externally rewarding and empowering. Thus, the chapters in this half of the book are shorter, much more "how-to" focused, and designed to really give you the exact blueprint that I used and have helped thousands of others use to make a successful transition from job living to dream living. Disclaimer: this material is not a get-rich-quick scheme, nor is it a rags-to-riches infomercial formula that only works for a special few. It's the truth, and it works. My friend, I want you to know that you are walking into this chapter loaded with a lot of powerful revelation from the previous chapters, and hopefully you are now armed and ready to make this thing happen.

YOU'RE HIRED!

Let me ask you a few opening questions.

- Do you want to spend more quality time with your family and friends?

- Do you want to be paid more for the value that you bring to your work?

- Do you see yourself calling the shots instead of having the shots called to you?

- Do you see yourself providing a service to others while being paid well for it?

- Do you want to determine your income instead of it being assigned to you?

- Do you have the passion, purpose, and potential to lead your life effectively?

- Do you want to become all that you feel you already are?

Well, if you answered yes to most or all of these questions, then it's time that you hire yourself! It's time for you to begin the process of transitioning. Nine times out of ten when you work for someone else, their primary mission and goal is *not* to make you financial free and independent. They want to get your skills, knowledge, ability, creativity, and ideas for as little as possible because your salary is directly affecting their bottom-line profits. So what you have to do is make the decision that you will hire yourself! The wealthiest people in the world are all entrepreneurs. Who are entrepreneurs? Entrepreneurs are people who hire themselves to provide a product or service of value to this world. They don't make wages; they make profits in exchange for those products and services. Period. Entrepreneurs are people who take chances on themselves and their ideas, inventions, concepts, music, talent, abilities, gifts, and so forth. We are now living in the age of the entrepreneur—the creative age. So it's time you make a decision to hire you! I did. By the way, did you know that every ten seconds someone in the United States starts a business? That's right. Every ten seconds someone takes that faithful step of hiring themselves. The future has never looked brighter for people who want to hire themselves. And I am not telling you what I think; I am telling you what I have lived and studied.

> There will be more than 10 million new millionaires in the United States alone created between 2006–2016. Prime candidates are those people who are in direct selling, technology, home-based business, product distribution, or the wellness field.
> —Paul Zane Pilzer Economist, Trend Forecaster, and best-selling author of *The Next Millionaires*

I hired myself in 1998 as a sole proprietor. As a motivational speaker, I would accept fees to speak at various events for high schools, colleges, community groups, and churches. After I graduated from Florida State with my master's degree, I moved my business back to my hometown of Tampa, Florida. I took the corporate consulting job in the middle of 2000 and began working. You know the story: I got let go and strategically took a dream job position at the University of South Florida (USF). I will share the hard numbers of this dream job and how I landed it in chapter 7. But what you don't know is that my real transition began during the four months that I went unemployed after my corporate job and before I started working at USF. I decided that I wanted to transition from being a corporate consultant to hiring myself to become a full-time professional speaker and author. I started with where I was and made a plan to transition. What about you?

Where Are You Right Now?

Tell me a little about yourself. I want to be clear as to who you are and where you are in your life right now. As much as I want to know this, it's critical that you know it and understand it.

» What do you do for employment?

_____

» How much money do you earn annually?

_____

» Do you like what you do for a living?

_____

» How much of your time does your current position take up?

_____

» Do you wish you could invest more time in your dream?

_____

» On a scale from 1 to 10, one being not bad enough to try and ten being so bad that you'll do whatever it takes, how bad do you want to transition?

_____

» On a scale from 1 to 10, one being not that tired and ten being fed up, how tired are you of your current situation?

_____

Where Do You Really Want to Be?

» What is your dream/calling?

_____

» Do you personally know people who have achieved this dream?

_____

» How much money do you initially want to earn doing this?

_____

» How much money do you ultimately want to earn doing this?

_____

» How much of your time each week are you willing to invest?

_____

» Do you have the support of friends, family, and/or colleagues?

_____

» Is this dream of yours a "should," an "ought to," or a "MUST"?

_____

» On a scale from 1 to 10, one being not that bad and ten being superbad, how bad do you want this dream?

_____

Great job! OK, now we are getting somewhere. My last question is, tell me why you want this dream. Why this dream, why you, and why now?

_____

_____

_____

_____

_____

Excellent! Now understand this powerful point. The information that you provided above serves as your gasoline. You are about to begin a life-transforming journey, and you need to know where you are and where you want to end up. You need a vehicle, and you need fuel. Your reasons—your why—is your fuel. The people who make it, those who succeed, all have fire-burning reasons why. Those who fail didn't have enough gas; they didn't have strong enough reasons for why they could not give up and why they had to achieve their dream no matter what. The reason why you will succeed is because of your why!

> There are two primary choices in life: to accept conditions as they exist, or to accept the responsibility for changing them.[2]
> —Denis Waitley

WHATEVER YOU WATER ... GROWS

It is vital for you to understand that during this time of transition, whatever you water is what will grow, just as the previous quote explains. Sounds a lot like something we talked about in chapter 3 called living life by default versus living life by design. You can either accept your life the way it is now, in the current occupational and financial situation that you're in now, or you can choose to change it into what you want it to be. However, it's important for you to know that while choices are critical for success, once you decide, you need to act! Once you decide to transition in the mind, you must then go there in the body! And this is where the real magic happens. See, most people do decide! They say, "Yes, I want to be an entrepreneur. I want to own my own business and start taking a leadership role in my future!" However, what typically happens is that their actions don't line up with that new choice, so they continue to manifest sameness instead of manifesting change and difference.

Look at what you want as a dream seed in the ground. Look at where you are as that same seed in the ground, just a few yards away. Look at positive thoughts, intelligent and consistent actions, and right relationships as the water that you must pour onto those seeds to make them grow into more of what they already are. As long as you water where you are, the same seed—with all of your time, energy, attention, focus, and finances—you are simply going to harvest more of the same! But the moment you start watering your dream seed with the right thoughts, the right actions, and the right relationships, and you do this consistently and persistently, that dream seed will start harvesting into a paid, full-time calling with benefits and tax breaks! Hello, somebody! It's 100 percent possible! Every day that you wake up, you have choices as to what you will water and what you won't water. The key is to learn how much you water your job and dream to allow yourself to transition effectively. This is an art, and I am going to teach you that art form. To put your understanding of this concept to the test, please list for me below five things you can do right now to start watering your dream seed. Need a hint? Some of the answers can come simply by remembering some of the friends of your potential. (For example, finishing this book is a great way to water your dream seed. Now list a few more!)

1. _____

    _____

2. _____

    _____

3. _____

    _____

4. _____

_____

5. _____

_____

MY TWO THEORIES OF TRANSITION

Over the years, I have asked tons of people how they would go about transitioning from their job to their dream. And over the years, I have gotten a wide variety of answers—some good and some crazy. However, almost all of the strategies I have heard and used fall neatly into either two theories of transition. These transition theories have to do with the rate and intensity with which you will make the shift in your life. Make no small deal about this. Transitioning from your job to your dream is probably one of the biggest decisions and action steps you will ever make.

The leap-frog theory

This theory, as it sounds, subscribes to the notion that you should just leap off the tree, cliff, or mountain and grow your wings on the way down. Some people believe that as soon as you believe in yourself and your dream enough to jump out on nothing, you will land on something solid. I have seen this theory hold true for a select few, yet it has left an overwhelming majority in the financial hospital of knee-deep debt, foreclosures, and bankruptcy filings. Some people need the emergency of leaping from the tree (job) 100 percent before they do the only thing they can do—flap their wings (talents) and fly (produce). This is a very aggressive and very risky approach. It occurs when people quit their jobs with no plan, no goals, and no direction. But they know for sure that they didn't want to do what they were doing for another second longer. This theory also kicks in when people are laid off or fired. But instead of leaping, they get kicked out of the tree. That is exactly what happened to me. I went from a fifty-thousand-dollar salary to nothing in one day! The next day I got up and made a vow to never let my destiny be determined by someone else again. I got up immediately and started writing my first book and building my speaking business. The rest is history. I believe that sometimes when you are

> Don't wait. The time will never be just right.[3]
> —Napoleon Hill

kicked out of the nest by life's situations, that's simply God's way of letting you know that you are ready to fly, even though you don't know it!

Sometimes it takes extreme hardship and emergency situations to move people. You need to know what it takes to get you moving toward your dream. Let me help you. Don't wait for life to act on you. You act on life. You will be much more successful that way. Don't wait for the carpet to be pulled out from under you before you begin to build a solid foundation underneath that carpet to hold you up. Begin preparing right now!

The Tarzan theory

The other theory of transition, and my personal recommendation, is what I call the "Tarzan theory." This theory suggests that it's better to hold on to a good thing until a great thing comes along. This theory is one of systematic, strategic progression from one stage in your life to the next. This school of thought is more gradual and less aggressive. The process is much more involved, detailed, and complex. It involves vision, focus, delayed gratification, continual preparation, mentorship, goal achievement, and building your dream line upon line and precept upon precept. This is my own personal recommendation for the best and wisest way to make a smart transition from your job to your dream. I call it the Tarzan theory because if you've ever watched the movie, TV show, or cartoon, you remember how Tarzan moves through the jungle. He swings from one vine to the next so fluidly and intentionally. He does not let go of one vine until he has a solid grip on the next one. This allows him to move quickly and systematically through the jungle and get to his destination successfully. You can do the same thing. Let me teach you how.

The rest of this book focuses on implementing the Tarzan theory throughout your transition from job living to dream living. This approach recommends keeping your day job while building your dream on the side until your dream is self-sustaining enough to support you and your family full-time. That reminds me of another point. Your decision between these two theories of transition should be weighed and considered heavily with the following factors of your life in mind.

- Age: What season of life you are in—your learning, earning, or retirement years?

- Marital status: Are there spouses, children, or other family members directly affected by your actions?

- Financial situation: Do you have the ability financially to step out on your dream?

- Experience level: Do you know enough about your dream industry to launch?

- Educational status: Do you have the credentials needed or personally desired to attain your dream?

You may be able to be a little more risky and choose the leap-frog theory if you are single, have little or no debt, are young enough to reenter the workforce (in the event of failure), have no major financial goals pending (like buying a house), and have a fair amount of experience. That leap will be much safer than one with the exact opposite scenario in play.

One last point about the Tarzan theory: just because it is less aggressive and more systematic and strategic does not mean that it will take forever. You can transition between your job and your dream using the Tarzan theory in a period of one to five years. I did it in two years. It all depends on the magnitude of your dream, the magnitude of your variables, and the magnitude of personal time and money that you are

> If you don't design your own life plan, chances are you'll fall into someone else's plan. And guess what they may have planned for you? Not much.[4]
>
> —Jim Rohn

willing to put on the line to make it happen for yourself. I have close friends who made the Tarzan transition within one year. So, in truth, it's really up to you. Each person's transition approach will be different. That's why we offer Job-to-Dream Transitional Coaching and Seminars! To learn more about them, visit us online at www.DelMcNeal.com. But finish this book first, because you are getting hours of coaching right now for the small price you paid for this book. What a deal!

The Tarzan theory gets you from point A (your job) to point B (your dream):

- On good terms with your past employer

- With little financial pressure placed on your dream

- With the education and credentials necessary to facilitate the dream

- With a strong partial client base and/or business already booked for your dream

- With a business and marketing plan in place to carry your dream to higher levels

- With solid financial structure for your dream that you and your family can trust

- With growth potential, motivation, and drive to live your dream daily!

A NOTE ABOUT THE RIGHT JOBS

Now, let me take a commercial break and say that there is nothing at all wrong with having a job. I know in chapter 2 I hit you pretty hard with "Whoever Told You to Job" material. All of that is true and correct, but remember, I told you that there are three types of jobs. Do you remember what they are? Dead-end jobs, stepping-stone jobs, and dream jobs. Well, in the grand scheme of things, dead-end jobs should be avoided at all costs. But stepping-stone jobs and dream jobs should be embraced, utilized for their purpose, and then moved on from. If you recall, I got my first official tax-paying job at age fourteen. I was a package executive at a local grocery store, and I was the best package executive—bag boy—they'd ever had!

The truth is that we all have to start somewhere, and the right types of jobs are the best places to start. There is a key difference between jobs and dreams. In addition, if done correctly, working the right types of jobs can be the best boot camp that your dream could ever have!

THE POWER AND PURPOSE OF THE STEPPING-STONE JOBS

The right jobs provide you with structure, discipline, and exposure.

One major benefit of a job is that it provides us with structure. We have set days to work, set hours to work, set tasks to complete, and set pay for our services. This structure allows us to frame our lives around the safety, security, and structure that the job provides. The structure that jobs provide mandates that we discipline our daily behavior so that we may birth habits such as effective time management, project management, people management, and resource management. As we utilize these skills, we gain exposure to clients, competition, and the marketplace. We need this exposure to allow our gifts and talents to grow and develop.

The right jobs provide you with experience.

The second major benefit of a job is that it allows us to gain industry-specific experience—hands-on, working, demonstrable knowledge of a skill that has cash value in the marketplace. This experience over time gives us a solid confidence that our talents and gifts will flourish given a variety of client situations. We need these skills for advancement, salary increases, and solid competition within the changing workforce. Experience speaks on your behalf and communicates your ability to handle multiple client situations with professionalism and proficiency.

The right jobs teach you the professional and interpersonal skills necessary in today's marketplace.

Every job has an extrinsic task and an intrinsic character-building equivalent. For example, a grocery store bag boy is not just supposed to learn the kinesthetic movements of bagging groceries but also organizational and ergonomic negotiation, communication, customer service, leadership, teamwork, money management, work/life balancing, and listening skills. What intrinsic character-building skills is your job trying to teach you? Whatever those skills are, you will need to use them in your dream.

> Twenty years from now you will be more disappointed by the things that you didn't do than by the ones you did do. So throw off the bowlines. Sail away from the safe harbor. Catch the trade winds in your sails. Explore. Dream. Discover.[5]
> —Mark Twain

The right jobs provide monetary compensation for your time and effort.

We all need money! Your life will crash if you don't have cash. Life can be mean if you don't have any green. Get my point? Every day billions of people exchange talent for money. Jobs allow us to exchange our time, talents, and abilities for money, benefits, experience, and credibility. The stability of a biweekly check gives us the consistency needed to maintain our households.

The right jobs are emotionally low-risk opportunities for growth.

Many people who have not stepped out into their dream full-time would probably disagree with this statement. However, allow me to explain. Most jobs are emotionally low risk compared to dreams because your dream is very personal and interpersonal. You can emotionally distance yourself from your job and the people with whom you work. However, when it comes to your dream, that is 100 percent personal; you invest your entire heart when you go after your dream. Therefore, rejections and criticisms are taken much harder when they come from the dream than when they come from the job.

The right jobs are building blocks for greater pursuits.

Each job you take should build on the previous one. Each job you have teaches you powerful skills that you will need once you pursue your dream full-time. The dream is coming, but meanwhile, maximize your time and profit potential by allowing the right job to put you in the right position to launch you correctly into your destiny.

THE POWER AND PURPOSE FOR DREAMS

Dreams provide purpose, significance, meaning, and excitement to life.

Your dreams help you to understand your assignment on Earth, the reason why you are here, and the meaning behind your passions, pains, tears, and joys in life. Your dreams give you hope that tomorrow can be better than today. Your dreams confirm that your life makes sense. They comfort you when you feel rejected by the world and by your job.

Dreams provide you with hope and expectation.

Many times while doing their job, people daydream of doing something else with their lives. These interruptions are scheduled by your destiny to be reminders of your true calling in life. They are designed to be constant reminders that your life and your existence have a far greater weight of importance than your present task communicates to you. They are consistent reminders of how awesome you really are!

Dreams provide you with an outlet for your greatness to be born, and they allow others to be blessed by your life's mission.

Without your dreams, your potential would go untapped. You would continue to wear the mask of compromise and settle for the present paychecks that you have already outgrown. Dreams are the midwife of your greatness that usher in the travailing of the destiny that others will benefit from throughout the totality of your life and beyond. Your dreams confirm that your talents are not for you! Rather, they are entrusted to you to be used by you to benefit others.

Dreams solve a problem for someone.

When you flow in your dream, your gifting will solve a significant problem for someone else. Dr. Mike Murdock encourages that we pay close attention to the things that frustrate us, because these are the things that our gifting is assigned to solve. When you follow your dreams, you service a need for someone you may or may not even know. Your highest feelings of contribution to mankind come when you see the manifestation of significance that your gifting has on someone's life.

Dreams provide the largest monetary compensation for your time and effort.

Paychecks from your job are nice, but the only true place that your financial blessings are guaranteed is within your dream and destiny. I was blessed to be able to replace the income from my last job twice over when I stepped into my dream full-time. People pursue dreams not for money but for fulfillment. Because of the passion and excellence with which dreams are pursued, money is a reward for the impact those dreams make.

Dreams require 150 percent of you.

Make no mistake about it; your dream is going to cost you everything—all of your energy, creativity, emotions, finances, courage, faith, fortitude, and zeal. When you pursue your dream, you take everything related to your dream personal. Why? Because it's yours. It's literally a piece of you. You can easily disown a job, but a dream is birthed out of the reservoir of your embodiment. Therefore it's very personal. You will never cry over a job setback like you will a dream setback. You will never celebrate the victory you have at a job more than you will the victory you experience with your own dream.

Dreams are the only things that make sense out of the tenses of your life.

When you consider your past (ups, down, hurts, pains, and successes), your present (current challenges, stresses, and discoveries), and your future (goals, plans, and aspirations), your dreams are the only things that make the totality of your life experience seem worth it. A job will never give you the lasting feeling that your past, present, and future challenges are worth it.

THE SIX PEOPLE WATCHING YOU

As you begin to transition, I want you to be fully aware of the six different types of people who are watching you while you are making your moves. As you know by now, I am a tremendous movie fan. I always watch movies that have a motivational theme in them. Recently, I watched again *Rudy, Men of Honor, Remember the Titans,* and *Rocky.* After watching these compelling stories of people who succeeded against the odds, I immediately was inspired to write this.

I believe that there are six types of people who are always watching you when you are in pursuit of your dream. Whether close to you or far from you, these individuals are watching. Your success means something different to each of them. Live your dreams because you have an audience, even if you don't know it. Search for each of the following individuals in the grandstands of your Tarzan transition success story.

1. **Those who never believed in you or your dream in the first place.** These are sometimes family, friends, and folks from your past whose limited vision and negative attitude pour ice water on the fire of your dream. Your success will educate them that it's possible! In many cases, these people are folks who never achieved their dreams. Always remember, most people will never have a larger vision of you than they have of themselves. And since most people view you through the lenses of their reality, it's difficult for people who don't see much in themselves to see greatness in you. Succeed anyway. Hate is educational. It means that you are very special and unique. Those that hate you really are just intimidated by you.

2. **Those who always believed in you and your dream.** Your success validates and confirms their lifelong support. There are people in your life right now who, no matter what you have done, said, or experienced, have always believed in you. These people in your life are worth more than any material possession you could ever have. Tyler Perry calls them the roots to your tree! Keep these people close to you and even closer to your dreams! Know that these people will be few in number but massive in impact upon your life. In addition to looking for

these people in your life, make sure that you are this type of person in the lives of others.

3. **Those who have been in your life for a brief time but whose profound words motivated you to keep going when you felt like giving up.** I believe that there are two types of empowerment: instant and ongoing. Instant empowerment is what you get when you hear a great speaker, teacher, lecturer, preacher, or scholar and what they say immediately resonates with the inner parts of who you are. This can also happen by watching a movie, reading a book, or listening to a speech that transforms your thinking instantaneously. Ongoing empowerment is when that immediate change is so profound that you keep that thought or concept with you through your day-to-day life and apply it to your routine life situations. Your success is a testament to the power of instant and ongoing empowerment. Sometimes the people who will make the greatest impact on your life and help you the most with your transition from your job to your dream are people with whom you have had brief encounters.

4. **Those who are neutral about your dream.** They don't really know you well enough to support you or discourage you; however, they are in position to promote, endorse, and accelerate your ultimate calling and dream. Life is full of people who are hot for your success or cold for it. However, there are also a ton of folks out there watching you and are lukewarm about your success. They are on the fence. The jury is still out as to whether or not they really believe in you. So guess what? To those people, you have some proving to do. My mother used to always say, "I can show you better than I can tell you!" Meaning, actions speak much louder than words. For these people, the proof is in the pudding. Even Scripture reminds us that people judge trees by the fruit that they produce. So the key for these people is to let your actions win them over to your side. The good thing about this type of person is that their unbelief can challenge you to produce. The bad thing about this type of person is that if they are exposed

to your dream too early, their lukewarm (wishy-washy) attitude can come across very cynical and jaded to you, causing negative energy that your dream does not need.

5. **Those who are living their dreams over again through your experience.** They want to see you capitalize on their mistakes. Your success is proof of the fact that it could have happened for them. In an odd way, when you succeed, they succeed. This type of person kept in check can be a great asset to your dream because although they are living vicariously through you, they sincerely don't want to see you make the same mistakes they did. They want to see you go further than they did, so they push you and really try to take care to see that you don't fall into the same traps they did. On the opposite side, however, this person can take their vicarious living to the extreme by pushing you too hard and by trying to make you think exactly the way they think. This person can become very selfish and can sabotage your success as a sick way of gaining comfort in the fact that they did not make it, and you did not either. Remember, misery loves company, and there is nothing more miserable than looking back over your life with a bunch of regrets. Monitor this person carefully; they can be a great liability or a great asset.

6. **Those who are coming behind you who need your success story to blaze a trail of possibility and opportunity for them.** Always remember that you are a trailblazer. Someone out there is watching you to see if what they want to do can really be done. They are not where you are in life yet, but they have the potential to become the same thing that you want to become. However, before they take their step of faith, they are looking at you to see if you sink or swim. You are the example, and in their life, you are the leader, the mentor, and the role model. In my profession, I meet people all the time who want to become professional speakers and authors. They tell me story after story of how they have watched my career grow and how they have seen me come out of bad situations and admired my

ability to keep on climbing. Trust me, there is probably someone you work with right now, a young person in your community, a friend on MySpace, a family member you don't talk to, a child of yours, or even a neighbor who is watching you step out in faith to live your dreams. They are scared to walk out on the water, so they are letting you be the guinea pig. That's OK. Show them that it's possible. After all, that's the blessing of leadership!

No matter who you are or where you are in life right now, always remember that people are watching you. Each one of these people is sitting back and studying your life, your actions, your decisions, your accomplishments, your valley experiences, and your mountaintop successes. So put on a show! Now that we have identified those who are for you and those you are against you, use *all* of them as fuel to get you closer to your destiny. Each relationship during this powerful transition is getting you one step further from your job and one step closer to your dream. Congratulations!

CHAPTER SUMMARY

EIGHT POINTS TO PONDER
DURING YOUR TRANSITION

1. Realize that it's time to hire yourself! You take chances on everything else, so why not take a chance on you? Look at your résumé, your education, your experience, your network of relationships, your vision, and your dream, and shake your own hand and say, "You're hired!"

2. Remember that the gap between where you are now and where you want to be professionally is your entrepreneurial potential. Close that gap by doing the things today that others won't do so that you can have the things tomorrow that others won't have—like freedom, choices, growth, limitless creativity, and autonomy.

3. Whatever you water is what will grow. Water your present, and you will harvest more of it. Water your future, and it will blossom into your destiny right before your very eyes.

4. The Tarzan theory states that you hold on to a good thing until a better and more progressive thing comes along. Your transition needs to be strategic. Be willing to leave the good to go for the great.

5. Working the right type of job can be the best boot camp that you can have for your dream.

6. Warning! Once you begin the transition process, you will no longer fit! You won't fit where you used to be because those people are happy working jobs. You won't fit where you want to be because those people are living their dreams. It's OK; just get

comfortable with being a little uncomfortable and not fitting in perfectly for a little while.

7. The purpose and power of jobs are good, but the purpose and power of dreams are far greater and much more rewarding in every way imaginable.

8. Wave. Wave at the six different types of people who are watching you live your dreams right now. Stay away from the negative ones, and keep the positive ones close to you!

CHAPTER 7

HARNESSING THE POWER
OF THE DREAM JOB

No one should negotiate their dreams. Dreams must be
free to fly high. No government, no legislature, has a
right to limit your dreams. You should never agree to
surrender your dreams.[1]

—Rev. Jessie Jackson

Buckle your seat belt and get ready for a powerful ride! Get your pen and highlighter in hand, and let's move because this is going to go fast. Each chapter from here on out is short, to the point, and full of great ideas that you can use now to transition from where you are to where you really want to be!

Consider the diagram below.

For most people, the gap between their current job and their lifetime dream is so great that they never even attempt to get from one to the other! What a tragedy!

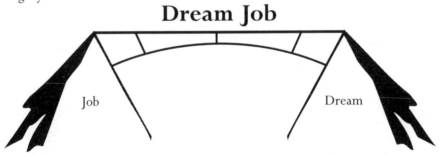

Dream Job

Job   Dream

However, you and I know better. You see, we know that there is a large gap between your job and your dream, but we also know that the bridge between your job and your dream is . . . *a dream job!*

HOW USF BECAME MY DREAM JOB

During the four months that I was unemployed before starting my career position with the University of South Florida (USF), I made several major decisions. I believe every job-to-dream transitioning person must make each one of these decisions in their own specific industry and in their own specific way.

1. I decided that never again would I allow my destiny to be 100 percent in the hands of someone else.

2. I decided that I was going to get in the driver's seat of my own life and career and begin to make things happen on my terms, not other people's.

3. I decided that I was going to be a full-time professional speaker and best-selling author one day. I was intentional about it and aligned my thoughts and actions with that decision.

4. I decided to change my company's status from sole proprietor to S corporation so that I would take it more seriously and begin to take more advantage of the tax benefits.

5. I decided that I needed a special type of job that would be the bridge that would get me from former corporate consultant to full-time speaker and author, while allowing me to provide for my family and myself.

6. I decided that whatever that job was going to be, I would only be there temporarily. I gave myself two years to transition, and I was intentional about making it happen in two years.

7. I decided that no matter what that job was, I was going to do it with quality and excellence, but whenever I was not on the job, I would be watering my dream. Nights, weekends, lunch

breaks, holidays, vacations, and daily drive time all belonged to my dream, not my job.

8. I decided that my dream was worth the sacrifice of my time and that I would do whatever was necessary to manifest my dreams in a two-year period. I made a choice to market myself as if I already was the thing that I wanted to be. So I didn't wait for others to start calling me a speaker; I started calling myself a speaker, writing my first book, and doing the things that speakers do! Don't wait for others to validate and affirm you. You do all that yourself, and let the praise and celebration of others be your gravy!

These powerful decisions framed my mind-set during the four months that I was unemployed. During that time, I had a variety of options. I could have found another job as a consultant or worked in a plethora of different career fields just to get money. But money was not the only thing I needed or looked for in my transitional job. I needed much more than just a paycheck. I felt that I needed to work in a place that would be consistent in similitude to the environment of my dreams.

> People are always blaming their circumstances for what they are. I don't believe in circumstances. The people who get on in this world are the people who get up and look for the circumstances they want, and, if they can't find them, make them.[2]
>
> —George Bernard Shaw

I did the Monster.com thing and sent out over four hundred job requests over the four months, but I did not get selected for the type of job I really wanted. See, jobs are everywhere, but dream jobs are special and require a little more finesse to secure. One day I was talking to a graduate school friend of mine who worked at USF in the special department called Organizational Development and Training (ODT). She told me that she was getting ready to move back to Tallahassee to be with her boyfriend and take a new corporate career position. She also told me that she thought I would be perfect to take her place in ODT at USF. After all, we both had the exact same master's degree, both graduated from FSU at the same time, and both had worked for and been released from top consulting firms. I was very interested in the position because she recommended it so highly and because it was in a university setting, which is much different and more relaxed and flexible than a corporate consulting environment. Before coming in for the interview, my friend warned me that the position paid less than what I was making in corporate, but that it was somewhat negotiable and the environment would be perfect for me, considering what she knew my goals were of wanting to become a full-time speaker someday.

> **Your mint is hidden behind your meant!**
> —Delatorro L. McNeal, II

Short story shorter, I went in for the interview with the director and assistant director of ODT. We hit it off immediately, and the connection was instant. However, one of the biggest benefits of the dream job came during the negotiation part of the interview. Back then, my position was paying forty thousand dollars a year plus benefits, which was great, but I was accustomed to making fifty thousand in corporate. So during the interview I requested that since I was going to be taking a ten-thousand-dollar pay cut, I would like to have a four-day workweek with one day per week off, and that each week, that day could fluctuate based on my speaking engagements calendar. So in other words, I would work four ten-hour days and have one day each week off. They agreed, and I signed the deal that same day! I knew that I had just landed my dream job!

THE MAGIC OF PART-TIME

Consider what just happened. I was able to negotiate more time for my dream while working my dream job. I signed on with USF full-time, but I created time to pursue my speaking dream part-time. And that's part of the magic of the dream job. Done correctly, it empowers and enables you to have the best of both worlds. So on nights, weekends, and that one day per week that I had off, I relentlessly pursued my speaking dream. Although my speaking career was part-time, when I was working on it, I treated it like it was full-time. I did not treat my part-time business like it was a part-time business. I treated it like a full-time business, and that's why it grew into what I treated it like. You have to do the same thing. So how much money did I make, and how long did it take me to transition? I know that's what you want to know. Well, here it goes. Applying everything I am teaching you in this book, from the introduction all the way through to the very last chapter, here is what happened.

I set a goal in 2002 to earn part-time the same money that I earned full-time working at USF. I know that sounds like an aggressive goal, but remember, I only gave myself two years, so I did not have time to play it safe. I had already been speaking as a gift and as a business for several years by this time, but now I was taking it "do-or-die" serious! So in 2002, while USF was paying me $40,000 full-time, part-time in my business I earned $43,000. I was amazed! I made $3,000 more in my first really serious year speaking part-time than I did at USF on salary working full-time. I knew then that my transition was working. Now, if you think about it, my first year after being let go from corporate and making $50,000 there, I was able to bounce back and earn a combined income of $83,000 by calling my own shots and working my dream and my dream job. All my family's benefits were covered by USF, and I was using the income from both my dream job and my business to pay off some personal debts and get my finances in order.

Going into 2003, I set an even bigger goal. In January of 2003, I set a goal of earning $100,000 part-time speaking while still maintaining my USF salary position of $41,000. They gave me a $1,000 raise the second year. Remember when I told you in previous chapters that your real income is found within your purpose, passion, and dream and not necessarily in a job? Well, this is living proof of that fact. So in my second year at USF, while earning $41,000 working full-time, I made $115,000 working part-time in my speaking and publishing business. My dream income had replaced my dream job income twice over, and that is when I decided to leave and launch out in speaking and publishing full-time. USF was one of the best career experiences I could have ever had in my life. Each day, I was working in an environment that helped to further prepare me for my dream. In 2004, which was my first full-time year speaking without the USF income, I earned $200,000 by the end of the year. Do you see how I used the dream job of USF ODT to intelligently and strategically transition myself from where I was to where I really wanted to be? Here's a diagram for further clarity.

Year	USF Dream Job	My Dream	Income Difference Dream-Over-Job	Total Income
2002	$40,000	$43,000	$3,000 1st year	$83,000
2003	$41,000	$115,000	$74,000 2nd year	$156,000
2004	-	$200,000	-	$200,000
2005	-	$230,000	-	$230,000

The quote on page XXX is so very true. The real income that you are supposed to be earning (your mint) is hidden behind the thing you are ultimately supposed to be doing with your life (your meant). By now, I should not have to say this, but I will for clarity: I did not share these numbers with you to brag or to impress you, because in truth they don't impress me. However, I do share them with you to impress upon you and inspire within you the reality that you can transition from your job to your dream, using the power of a dream job. Now some people might say that the income I am sharing here is not all that much, but that is relative. I never promised to show you how to make millions, because in truth, not everyone will become a millionaire. However, what I have shown you is that it's possible to make great money doing what you love and systemically transition from job living to dream living effectively. Let me ask you a few quick questions.

> Don't let the folks you hang with be your hang up. But rather allow the people you connect with to be your hook up. For the people with whom you network will ultimately determine your net worth!
> —Delatorro L. McNeal II

How long would I have had to stay working in corporate to get my income from $50,000 to $230,000 dollars? How long would I have had to work at USF, with my annual increases of $1,000 per year, to climb from $40,000 to $230,000? Most people in my keynotes, seminars, and coaching sessions reply with ten years, twenty years, some even say thirty-plus years. However, by harnessing the power of the dream job and working both smart and hard, I was able to transition in two years and earn the great income doing what I love! Remember in chapters 1 and 2 I told you that the real definition of success is doing what you love to do, the thing that you were born to do, and finding somebody who will pay you to do it.

Eight Facts About the Dream Job That Is Waiting for You to Discover It

1. **Your dream job will require you to use the same skills needed in your dream.** The dream job will have you using similar skills as the ones you will need in order to function at full capacity in your dream. This gives you daily practice opportuni-

ties to further hone your skills. At USF, I was training, speaking, writing curriculum, facilitating team building, and supervising technology interns. I do all that and much more in my dream.

2. **Your dream job will pay you to practice your dream skills.** The employer of your dream job may not know this, but while they are paying you to solve a problem for their organization, they are also compensating you to practice your skills on them. This is a win-win deal! This pay will allow you to maintain and slowly eliminate bills so that you can be more financially free as you move into your dream.

3. **Your dream job provides you with contacts that will help you when you leave.** There are people whom you will meet while performing within the dream job who will serve as great customers, clients, contacts, mentors, mentees, and colleagues once you step out into your dream full-time. Network like it's nobody's business while you are working at your dream job. However, be aware of competition and confidentially issues.

4. **Your dream job provides you a degree of scheduled flexibility to begin to focus some time toward your dream.** Time is your friend when in transition from your job to your dream. The dream job that awaits you will require your focus and attention. However, it will also give you routine opportunities to focus on your dream. If you recall, in my dream job I negotiated a four-day workweek. That was ten-hour days, four days a week. That always gave me one day a week *off* to focus 100 percent on my dream. It was great! Les Brown always says, "You don't get in life what you want; you get what you negotiate!"

5. **Your dream job will provide you with medical benefits to cover you and your family during the transition period.** For many people, this is critical. A steady dream job will give you the comfort of a nice benefits package that will cover and protect you and your family while you get paid to practice your dream. You can work day to day with the security of knowing

that if anything happens, you and your family have benefits to go to the doctor, dentist, hospital, and anything else that may arise.

6. **Your dream job provides a level of employment credibility so that you can accomplish your major financial goals.** Listen, this is huge. When you want to buy a home, a car, or office space, most lending institutions look at brand-new businesses with very strict guidelines. In fact, in order for your new business's income to even count with most lenders, you need at least two full years of tax returns. Your dream job provides the steady income plus the established name recognition needed for you to secure major purchases while in transition to your dream. Remember that your dream, while big to you, is still a baby in many ways to most people. You want to take as much financial pressure off of yourself and your dream as possible in the beginning. For example, I bought cars, paid off credit card debt, paid for computers with cash, and bought a brand-new home while still at my dream job; then I made the transition after the closing. This made life much easier for us. We will talk more about this later.

7. **Your dream job builds your confidence in your skill set for your dream.** For some people, the transition from job to dream is not financial. Lack of skill is the issue. Some people don't feel competent enough to step out on their dream full-time and make good money doing it right away. Well, if that's you, you need a season or several seasons of additional preparation. You need a boot camp experience. The dream job further assists you with that. Remember, it pays you to practice!

8. **Your dream job can provide you with lasting business and personal relationships even after your transition.** The people whom I met and worked with on my dream job are lifers. You know, those people who you just know will always be a part of your life in some way or another throughout the duration. I met some of the best-quality people this world can make at my dream job.

FIVE POWERFUL RESOURCES FOR FINDING
AND LANDING YOUR DREAM JOB

It is very possible to do what you love and get paid for it, be it as your own business or as a great career position that you would consider your calling or dream! However, in order to land your dream job, there are some key sources and resources that I would highly advise you to maximize.

1. **Relationships.** Connections are key. It has been said that as high as 90 percent of regular jobs, and dream jobs especially, are *not* advertised on the Internet or in major publications. It is very important that you connect with the right people in the industry of your passion and let people know that you are looking for a dream job opportunity. I landed USF because of a relationship, not an ad or a job posting. It was simply people power! Relational capital is very important to your success in landing your dream job.

2. **Industry-specific publications.** Go visit the local bookstore, and just spend some time really searching for magazines that are specific to your industry. While writing this book, I was coming back from Utah to Tampa on a flight, and while passing through the airport, I saw a magazine that had a major article titled "Landing Your Dream Job," so I picked it up. The magazine was specifically for people who like outdoor/recreational careers, but it was full of powerful resources for people who have a passion for that. So whatever your industry is, find publications that focus on what you love to do, and see what dream job opportunities exist inside.

3. **Conferences and conventions.** Every major career field or industry has some type of an association and/or conference that enables the professionals within that industry to come together, network, be inspired, and share best practices. Find the right conferences in your industry, and invest in a trip to go meet face-to-face with people who do now what you want to do soon! I tell new speakers all the time that a great place to network and meet other speakers, authors, and experts is NSA, the National Speakers Association. "Place yourself in venues that facilitate in-person

networking," says Katharine Hansen, author of *A Foot in the Door: Networking Your Way Into the Hidden Job Market.*[3] "In a survey for my book, the top two networking venues were professional associations and volunteer organizations."

> There is nothing like a dream to create the future.[4]
>
> —Victor Hugo

4. **Online resources**. The Internet is here to stay. Google what you want, and it will appear! Here is just a sampling of the thousands of online sites that can help you!

- VocationVacations.com: pay to try out your dream career for a weekend.
- DreamJobCoaching.com: get expert advice on how to land your dream job.
- Headhunters.com: work with recruiters who will personally help to match you with the right career opportunities.
- TheLadders.com: great Web site for executives looking for one-hundred-thousand-dollar jobs.
- CareerChange.com: great for anyone looking for dream jobs paying over $100,000.
- CareerBuilder.com: great for people from all ages to help find great careers.
- Jobing.com: great for anyone wanting to find occupations within their local surroundings.
- Salary.com: cost of living indexes, salary ranges for various careers, and searches.
- ExecuNet.com: a trusted executive network committed to the career-long success of executives earning one hundred thousand dollars a year.
- LiveCareer.com: take a free career interest test to determine what you want.
- Monster.com: get career and résumé advice, post your résumé, attend job fairs.

5. **Career/job fairs and expos**. Go where the jobs and careers are. Meet the people who are looking for you. Put yourself in the right

environment at the right time, and you never know what could happen. The only major challenge with fairs and expos is the cattle-call methodology that tends to be the norm in most of these venues. Make yourself stand out in a really positive way. Remember that at these events, less is more. Spend less time going to every booth, and invest the most time at the booths of the organizations that you really want to connect with. The name of the game at an expo or fair is to do your research in advance. Know who will be at the expo already and plan your strategy before you get there. Also, going with a friend/business colleague is another great idea because you can cover more ground that way.

SIX REMINDERS ABOUT THE DREAM JOB

1. **The dream job is not permanent.** Its purpose is not for you to be 100 percent comfortable. Why? Because you will never be 100 percent comfortable in something that is not your destiny. Don't get comfortable in your dream job. It is temporary. It is a bridge to something bigger and better. Use it for that purpose and that purpose only.

2. **Don't assume that the dream job is going to be easy.** Many people view dream jobs as all glitz and glamour with no issues and drama. All careers, all callings, all dream jobs have certain aspects that are not fun and enjoyable, but they are a part of the process. So take the good with the bad, and realize that although you love it, you may not feel like doing it all the time.

3. **The dream job does not birth your ultimate dream.** It simply prepares you and your environment for the dream to be born. Don't settle for the comfort that the dream job provides. Go all the way! Keep putting one foot in front of the other, and don't stop until you get to the other side of your bridge. USF was awesome, but it could not hold a candle to my dream. It simply couldn't because that was not its purpose. Its purpose was to enable me to transition, while also allowing me to make a massive impact upon the university at the same time.

4. **Maximize your time while in your dream job.** Don't procrastinate! Expect to work nine to five, then come home and work an additional two to four hours on your dream. Again, this dream job is a window of opportunity to build a silent empire while you are still benefiting from the stability that your dream job provides. I will tell you more about lunch breaks and what to do with them in the coming chapters.

5. **Keep a council of wisdom around you at all times during your transition.** Your wisdom council will help you predict and determine when your season at the dream job is ending. They will help you identify the final steps that need to be completed before your successful launch into your dream full-time.

6. **Never burn your bridges!** Always treat people with respect and with the knowledge that they could bless you in a special way sometime in the future. Just because you won't be in your dream job long does not give you license to burn a bridge as you exit. Be polite, be confidential with your various dream moves, and invite only those who believe in you to help with your dreams.

OK, so now that you understand the power of the dream job and how to go about landing it, please tell me in the space below what type of dream job would be best for you. What job/career opportunity can do for you what USF ODT did for me, and what steps are you going to begin to take to land it?

CHAPTER SUMMARY

EIGHT POINTS TO PONDER
DURING YOUR TRANSITION

1. Don't let the gap between your job and your dream stop you from success. Bridge that gap with a dream job.

2. Once you decide to land a dream job, don't just settle for any old job that just gives you a check, because you need much more than that!

3. Remember, you don't get in life what you want; you get what you negotiate. Make sure you get secure, win-win deals when you interview for your dream job.

4. Treat your part-time dream like it's a full-time dream, and watch it grow into the thing you treat it like.

5. Your mint is hidden behind your meant. Go after it. There is no shortage of money in this country. Go get what belongs to you financially.

6. The dream job pays you to practice your skills on an organization that needs your help in solving their problems. It's the best boot camp your dream can have.

7. Maximize relationships, publications, conferences, the Internet, and career fairs to help you land your dream job.

8. Use the dream job for its transitional purpose, and keep swinging from vine to vine until you land at your dream.

Section 3

TIPS for Stepping
Powerfully Into Your Dreams

CHAPTER 8

ATTITUDE TIPS

Attitude is a little thing that makes a big difference.
—Winston Churchill

WELCOME TO THE TIPS CHAPTERS! WILLIE JOLLEY, WHO IS ONE OF my mentors and dear friends, defines TIPS as Techniques, Ideas, Principles, and Strategies. The chapters that follow are loaded with all four of these. Each chapter includes a brief yet powerful pillar that will build the support under the bridge between your job and your dream. These items will empower you to immediately begin to take the necessary action steps that will put you on the fast track to living your dreams. The first pillar is attitude.

Dream Job

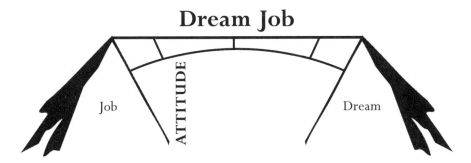

As you make the transition from your current job to your dream job to your ultimate dream, you are going to go through a variety of changes. These changes include: mental, emotional, financial, relational, spiritual, chronological, social, and entrepreneurial. However, as you negotiate all of these positive changes in your life, the one thing that needs to stay consistently strong and positive is your attitude!

ATTITUDINAL TIPS FOR
SUCCESS IN YOUR DREAM JOB

1. Recondition and program your mind for success.

This is the very first step to anything you want to do or create in your life. You can't achieve until you first believe. It's difficult to truly believe until you have reconditioned your mind and gotten rid of all the "stinkin' thinkin'" that says that you can't do it, you will fail, you can't make it, you don't have what it takes, and so on. Take out the trash! Set all that negative stuff out for the trashman to come pick up. You have to start each day believing in yourself and your dream because, remember, you will manifest whatever your most dominant thoughts are. You

> If you don't think every day is a good day, just try missing one.
>
> —Cavett Robert

will become what you think about consistently. Just as superior athletes have to condition their bodies and muscles for optimum performance in sports, superior people who want to live their best life right now must do the same thing. Create an atmosphere around you that consistently communicates to your mind consciously and unconsciously that you can succeed! Program your mind to think possibility!

2. Listen to something positive every day!

Change and transition are very exciting but very uncomfortable also. So it is imperative that you be as proactive as possible to keep your environment positive and empowering. I once heard in a speech that if you listen to something positive the first twenty minutes of your day, you will increase your productivity by 35 percent. Look at your mind and your heart as the hard drives of your life. If you install bad software, you will get bad performance and possibly even viruses. If you install quality and positive software, you will get great performance and longevity out of your machine. Well, the same is true of your day.

The reality is that each day you live is a magnificent creation. So use your power to create your days and not just have them! Each morning, play motivational tapes, CDs, DVDs, and videos, and read inspirational literature. This will shape your attitude early in the morning and help to set the bar high for your day. Don't read the newspaper and focus on a bunch of negative articles and stories about how bad things are in the world. Be informed, but stay positive! Your mind is just like a radio. Whatever station you tune it to are what programs it will play. If you tune a radio to country, of course country music comes out. If you tune it to R&B, gospel, smooth jazz, talk, or sports radio, the same thing will happen. You will get what programs are consistent with that station that you deliberately tune your radio to. Well, the same is true of your life. If you tune the frequency of your mind and thoughts to negative things and people, you will attract and manifest negative. However, if you tune it to positive things and the things that make each day beautiful, you will be amazed at what comes into and out of your life.

3. Read at least one book per month.

Do you know that the average American only reads one book per year? What a shame! While the average American is reading one book per year, the average self-made millionaire in America is reading one book per month! Readers are indeed leaders. Ask your mentors what books they are reading. Ask the people whom you admire in your chosen profession what books they have read so you can begin a personal and professional library. To get a current list of my top favorite books, visit my Web site at www.DelMcNeal.com, click on "Free Resources," and scroll down to "Delatorro's Must-Read Book List." Always invest in good material. If you are not disciplined enough to sit down and read the books, then buy them on CD, MP3, or audiocassette so that you can listen to them during your commute. Make sure that you are building a library of wisdom for yourself and your family. Always invest more in what goes in you (information, knowledge, wisdom) than what goes on you (clothes, perfume, makeup). I am not saying to not look nice and keep up with the current fashion. That's fine. However, make it your goal to invest in wisdom from other people that can transform your life and dreams forever. Don't do what I used to do, though. I got so caught up in buying new books that I had more books on my shelf than I could read. I would read one chapter, then go to the next book. I knew a little about each book but not a lot about any of them. Bad move! Focus on reading one book all the way through, then move to the next one. Create a system that allows you to complete them one at a time and then share them with others. I've always said that if you can learn for fifteen dollars what it took someone fifteen years to learn, you got a great bargain!

4. Post your goals, and read them daily.

I can't tell you how powerful this is! How can you hit a target you can't see? Better yet, how can you hit a target that you don't have? Truth is, you can't. You have to have a vision for where you want your life to go and goals to help guide you there. Live your life by vision, goals, and action—plain and simple. The people who are the most successful are the top 3 percent who have written goals they are working toward on a daily basis.[1] Create goals for *all* areas of your life and for each stage of your Tarzan transition process. Goals don't have to be annual. They can be goals for the month, week, day, or hour. Be as detailed as you need to be, and micromanage yourself if you need to, but get yourself to write what's in your head down on paper so you can read it and internalize it daily. Where should you post your goals? I will challenge you to post your written goals in your bathroom on your mirror or at eye level opposite your toilet. Why? Because this guarantees that you will see them daily for at least a few minutes. If you travel a lot like I do, put them in your wallet or purse, or save them as a text document on your phone or PDA. Psychologists say that the average human being processes about sixty thousand thoughts per day; therefore, you need to keep your goals in the forefront of your mind so that your goals are the beneficiary of the majority of your positive creative energy. Goals are a consistent reminder that you are closer than you think to realizing your dreams!

> The only disability in life is a bad attitude.[4]
>
> —Scott Hamilton

5. Watch empowering television and movies.

Do you know that the average American watches eight hours of television per day?[3] Meanwhile, the average self-made millionaire watches one hour of television per day, and it's usually something educational.[4] Input really and truly does determine output, my friend. So the first step is to limit your television watching to a few hours per day. Once you have done this, you will create more time to focus on your dream. Once you cut back on your hours in front of the TV, monitor the types of things you watch when you do turn on the TV. Try to focus on programs and movies that have moral value, teach empowering principles, and inspire your continued growth and development. "OK, Del. Are you saying I can't watch my favorite sitcoms?" No, trust me, I have my favorite shows just like anyone else. The key word here is *balance*. TV is very entertaining and informative, but don't allow it to make you lazy, lethargic, negative, bitter, or jealous of the opportunities that other people have. I suggest limiting it because when you're trying to transition from your job to your dream, each day counts. You need to invest your time in making your dreams happen rather than watching other people's dreams happen. Additionally, just as you should read and collect books, you should do the same with movies. Have a big library of movies that stimulate your mind, inspire your heart, and encourage your journey.

6. Take your megavitamins daily.

I know that you probably think I am talking about a pill that you pop each day, but actually I am not. Megavitamins are very important, and I recommend that you do what your doctor and/or health specialist recommends to maintain optimal health. However, I am referring to a different type of vitamin. You see, I have a variety of positive people in my life that I call megavitamins. These people serve multiple roles in my life, and they give me the daily dose of encouragement and support necessary to stay on top of my game. Just as a nutritional megavitamin gives you a plethora of nutrients, vitamins, and minerals all in one tablet or capful of liquid, the right types of positive people can do the same. For example, I have a megavitamin named Mr. Tye Maner. He is a professional speaker, trainer, author, and entrepreneur. He serves multiple roles in my life—friend, mentor, mastermind group member, fellow speaker, author, technology buddy, financial and entrepreneurial advisor, and just overall confidant. See,

> **Attitude is everything![5]**
> —**Keith Harrell**

you don't need hundreds of people in your life as long as you have a few who serve multiple roles. And just as he serves many roles in my life, I serve multiple roles in his life. To stay healthy during and after your transition from your job to your dream, you have to take your megavitamins daily and be a megavitamin for others as well.

7. Pour into someone else's dream.

This is one of the most powerful principles you can learn. Sometimes when you are focusing so much on making your own dreams happen, you can get tunnel vision. Because your focus is so narrow, you think, "My goals, my dreams, my purpose, my job, my visions, my ... my ... my!" Tunnel vision is important to have to eliminate distractions, and healthy selfishness is a good thing, but it is also very important for your attitude that you make it happen for someone else. Find someone whom you believe in, maybe someone whom you admire and respect, and help him or her or their organization become more successful. "Why, Del?" you may be asking. "Don't I have my own problems to worry about? Why deposit my time and energy into someone else's dream?" The reason why you want to do this is threefold.

1. It puts you in the environment of greatness.

2. It conditions you to understand that sometimes making your dreams come true happens indirectly through servanthood.

3. It exposes you to a much larger world of possibility, which expands your mind, proves that your dream is possible, and ultimately empowers your positive attitude.

The law of reciprocity states that what goes around comes around, and what is done to others will come back to you. Scripture even reminds us that what we make happen for someone else, God makes that and much greater things happen for us. It's like the boomerang theory. What you send forth will come back to positively impact your life. I met Les Brown because I was a servant. I met Willie Jolley because I was a servant. I met Bishop T. D. Jakes because I was a servant. I met Zig Ziglar because I was a servant. Dr. Stephen Covey, Fred Hammond, Dr. Mike Murdock, Maya Angelou, Dr. John Maxwell—the list goes on and on. I purposely put myself in the position to assist someone else with their goals and dreams, and in the process, my goals were achieved. Serve someone. Get behind someone else's vision. Push someone else to the next level. It will come back to bless your socks off.

> Attitudes are contagious. Are yours worth catching?[6]
> —Dennis and Wendy Mannering

8. Create a dream book, wall, or room in your house.

I got this helpful hint from one of my mentors, Dr. Mike Murdock. I have a room in my house that is 100 percent dedicated to my future, my business, my goals, my dreams, my accomplishments, my ideas, my support, and visions of the reality that I am trying daily to manifest. This room has pictures of me with great mentors whom I study under, letters of appreciation from past speaking events, my calendar for the month with goals, copies of past large and small paychecks from events, my degrees, wisdom quotes, pictures of great men and women whom I admire, vacations I want to take and have taken, the homes I want to live in someday, the types of cars and planes I want to travel in, and newspaper articles that I have been featured in. In that room, all things are possible! My dream room challenges me to pursue more, and it also encourages me that things will continue to get better and better. And whenever I get down about something, my negative attitude and I can't stay together in that room. One has to go, and since the room is permanent, my mind flip-switches to a renewed and refreshed perspective.

These are just eight simple TIPS that you can begin to implement into your life and that will impact your attitude in tremendous ways. As you transition from your job to your dream, your attitude is one of the most powerful things you need to guard.

CHAPTER SUMMARY

EIGHT POINTS TO PONDER
DURING YOUR TRANSITION

1. You will become what you think about! Thoughts become things, so think your way into whatever you want.

2. Remember your mind is like a radio. Tune it to the right stations, and you will attract great things into your life.

3. Readers are leaders. Read one book per month and apply what you learn.

4. Goals help to give your attitude the burst of momentum needed to keep you positive and excited from one success point to the next.

5. Input determines output. Garbage in equals garbage out. Excellence in produces excellence out. Watch empowering television that makes you feel good.

6. Identify and celebrate the megavitamins in your life, and be a megavitamin for others also.

7. Service is the greatest form of leadership. Help make someone else's dreams come true and watch that energy come right back to you.

8. Our minds love imagery, and we pursue what we see. So create and live in the sanctuary of your dream room, where all things are possible!

CHAPTER 9

SPIRITUAL AND EMOTIONAL TIPS

The most powerful weapon on earth
is the human spirit on fire.[1]
—Marshal Ferdinand Foch

THE POWER OF THE HUMAN SPIRIT IS PROBABLY THE MOST AMAZING THING on the earth! It's been said that the average human being has enough potential power, in terms of spirit energy, within them to light up an entire city for up to a week. That's amazing! We all are made up of three things—mind, body, and spirit! The spirit part of us is the part of us that is in direct connection to our Creator, God the Father. I believe the spirit part of each of us lives forever into eternity. Our bodies are just earth suits, and our minds are the things that control the earth suit and allow us, through the power of free will, to choose our future and create it daily. Our minds, as we have already discussed, play a huge part in our success. Without the right mind-sets, paradigms, concepts, ideas, strategies, and cognitive processes going on in the mind, we can't really produce the results we seek in life.

However, you can have all the book smarts there are in the world, but if you don't have will, determination, fortitude, tenacity, resiliency, courage, vigor, passion, drive, and expectation, which are functions of the spirit, you won't achieve real success! So here's where we add another pillar underneath our bridge from job living to dream living.

Dream Job

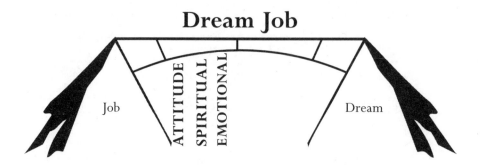

I remember hearing a speaker friend of mine, Professor Joe Martin, say in a speech, "Your 'I WILL' is always more powerful than your IQ!" So it becomes vital that we focus some time in this chapter talking about the power of the human spirit and various ways that we can stimulate it to greatness. At the same time, it's difficult to talk about spiritual TIPS of success without talking about emotions and the powerful role they play in our lives. Most highly spiritual experiences are very emotional experiences as well. They kind of go hand in hand. Our emotions are a powerful guidance system given to us by God to help us know when our thoughts, actions, and experiences are in alignment or out of alignment with our deepest desires and His deepest desires for us.

Emotions come in two categories: good and bad. Simply put, good emotions are those that you feel when you are in alignment with your deepest desires, hopes, and expectations. Bad emotions are those that you feel when you become misaligned with your ultimate goals, wants, and needs in life. Either way, all emotions serve us and give us signs, signals, and clues as to whether or not we are on track or off. Thus, managing and mastering our emotional states become the key to creating the success we want. As you transition from your job to your dream, know that it's going to take a significant toll on you spiritually and emotionally, but the TIPS I have for you over the next few pages will help you navigate this wonderful journey into the life you have always wanted.

1. Pray, meditate, and attract!

Praying is simply communicating with God through your spirit. That's it. It's connecting spirit to spirit with the Creator and going through a process of uploading and downloading information, requests, gratitude, petitions, concerns, fears, ideas, praise, adoration, visions, wants, expectations, and the like. This process of communicating with God frees us from having to shoulder the entire weight of the daily challenges we face in life. As you transition, you are going to have questions that people can't answer, and that's when you turn to God to get the clarity that you need. Remember when I decided to leave USF? Well, I was still on the fence about it until I heard a confirmation from God.

Prayer inspires, motivates, encourages, empowers, strengthens, refreshes, refocuses, and recharges us. We as human beings are just like cell phones. At the end of the day or after extensive use, we need to be recharged. Now, after a long day at work, you don't just rest your cell phone on the dresser and expect it to function at full capacity the next morning, do you? No! Why not? Because you understand that the cell phone needs to be plugged into an electrical source that is far greater and more powerful than it is in order to pull from that source and recharge itself. Well, my friend, we are the same way. We must recharge ourselves and refocus ourselves on our purpose and potential each day. Prayer allows us to do that. Develop a healthy prayer life, and watch how much more successful you become.

> The great awareness comes slowly, piece by piece. The path of spiritual growth is a path of lifelong learning. The experience of spiritual power is basically a joyful one.[2]
>
> —M. Scott Peck

The great thing about meditation is that it births focus. When I say prayer and mediation, please don't wig out on me, because I am not talking about some religious ritual. I am referring simply to dedicated quiet time to connect with yourself, God, and your goals. Whatever it is that you really want, begin to pray and mediate daily on that thing, and it will begin to manifest in your life. You will begin to attract into your life the people, places, things, and ideas that align with your prayers and mediation. Through the power of right thinking, feeling, being, and acting, you can attract just about anything into your life.

> Finally, brethren, whatsoever things are true, whatsoever things are honest, whatsoever things are just, whatsoever things are pure, whatsoever things are lovely, whatsoever things are of good report; if there be any virtue, and if there be any praise, think on these things.
>
> —Philippians 4:8

2. Express gratitude, and use the flip-switch!

One of the strongest attitudes and emotions you can ever express and live within is that of gratitude! Each morning, before you enter your day, just take a little time and mediate on the people, places, things, ideas, mind-sets, and heart-sets that you are grateful for. Whether things are going great in your life or not, you have something to be thankful for. If you have the ability to read this book, listen to it, or interpret it in some way, you have something special to be thankful for. What tends to happen is that because there are so many things to be negative about in this world and in our society, we tend to focus on the negativity and what we don't want and don't have. I would like to challenge you, and I know that this is easier said than done, but whenever you are in a mood or emotional state that is not positive and empowering, in the exact moment that you are feeling negative, immediately think of three things that you are grateful for. No matter how big or how small, if you consciously focus your mind on three things that are going right in your life at that time, you will be amazed at how you can flip-switch to the positive.

> Good, better, best.
> Never let it rest till
> your good is better
> and your better is best.
>
> —Author Unknown

I first heard of the flip-switch technique from Anthony Robbins, and then from Dr. Robert Anthony. Just like a light switch instantly turns light on and off in a room, we can do that same thing with our minds and our emotional/spiritual states. But it requires a commitment to catch yourself in the moment and make a shift to interrupt your existing pattern. Nobody can make you feel bad or negative all day long without your permission. Take control of your emotional states, and keep yourself feeling good about the many things going on in your life. For the things that you don't feel good about, take that as a sign from your emotions that you need to make a change! Wake up feeling grateful, and go to bed feeling grateful, and watch the blessings that come flooding your way.

> My brethren, count it all joy when ye fall into divers temptations; knowing this, that the trying of your faith worketh patience.
>
> —James 1:2–3

3. Don't allow "I don't feel like it" to ruin your dreams!

Remember this one thing, my friend: the entire world is run by people who "don't feel like it!" If you allow your feelings to determine whether or not you will get up each morning and go after your dream, you will starve. There will be many times when you don't feel like it. Do you think that Oprah always feels like being on camera? Do you think that Bill Gates always feels like talking about technology? Do you think that Denzel Washington always feels like acting or directing? Do you think that I always feel like speaking? Do you think that each time I came to the laptop to write this book, I was 100 percent excited about it? Think again! (Smiles!) This world is run by people who don't feel like it, but they do what needs to be done anyhow. I may not always feel like speaking, but once I start, the gift takes over, and greatness is born once again. Oprah may not always feel like being on camera, but the moment she begins interviewing a guest, her gifting takes over, and she creates a great show. My friend, don't allow how you feel to negatively impact your life. Command your body to fall in line with your positive mental and spiritual outlook toward your dream.

4. Always grow and contribute.

We talked briefly about this earlier in the book, but allow me to expound a little here. According to Anthony Robbins, there are six human needs.[3] The first four—certainty, variety, significance, and connection/love—are all needs of the personality. The last two needs—growth and contribution—are needs of the spirit! Your spirit needs to be ever expanding and evolving. You were made in the image and likeness of an ever-expanding God, so therefore you are ever expanding. Always place yourself in positions of growth. Don't allow jobs, careers, or callings to stop your growth and development. Never allow people—old friends, boyfriends, girlfriends, family members, spouses, or business colleagues—to keep you stagnant, because there are only two directions in life. Either you are growing, or you are dying! Grow, and grow daily. Additionally, the more you grow, the more you will have to give of yourself. The more you grow, naturally the wiser and more experienced you will become. This experience and wisdom needs to be passed down to others who are following in your footsteps. Many people think that contribution has to always come in the form of money, and although that is one way to contribute, it's not nearly the only way. We can and should always give of our time, talents, treasures, and resources. Think of it; the more you give, the more you are in position to receive!

5. Get comfortable with being stretched!

The purpose of your dream is to stretch you toward your destiny. It should be a constant reminder of how awesome you are and how much more awesome you can become. When making the transition between your job and your dream, you will be stretched. This includes your time; your ability to focus, multitask, and discern who should be in your life and who should go; your ability to keep quiet about your goals until you have attained them; and so many other things. Prepare to be challenged! Prepare to be emotionally and spiritually stretched. Prepare to be financially stretched. There will be times when you are moved to sow into the vision and dream of someone else while yours is still in the infant stage. That's OK! Sow that seed of money, time, or talent. Why? Because whatever you do to help someone else get his or her dream will be made possible for your dream in the future. Whatever you do to help someone else does not leave your life. It just enters your future to create an opportunity that you will benefit from later. So get comfortable being in a constant state of change. Your paradigm will be adjusting with each book that you read, each seminar you attend, each new milestone you achieve, and each new power relationship you establish. Your dream will continue to expand as you realize for yourself that "It's possible!" So instead of looking at change as a one-time thing, look at it as a continual refining process. Did you know that the average plane goes through over thirty thousand adjustments while in flight—including speed, cabin pressure, altitude, direction, and temperature? As passengers, we don't physically feel most of those adjustments, but they are necessary to ensure a safe transfer from where we are to where we want to be. You too will experience many adjustments along your journey of transformation from job living to dream living. Many won't be easy, but some will be a piece of cake. All of them will be working for your good. They will prepare you for greatness!

> Happiness cannot be traveled to, owned, earned, worn, or consumed. Happiness is the spiritual experience of living every minute with love, grace, and gratitude.
>
> —**Denis Waitley**

> All things work together for good to them that love God, to them who are called according to his purpose!
>
> —Romans 8:28

6. Pour into yourself.

I talked with you earlier in this chapter about how rechargeable the human spirit is. Our souls and spirits get tired and worn down by life and by transition. We must continue to pour into ourselves. Why? Because you can't pull anything out of an empty bag! As a speaker, author, consultant, and success coach, I am always pouring my positive energy out and into others. Whether it's through books, CDs, keynotes, seminars, interviews, coaching sessions, or otherwise, I am constantly pouring. As I pour my greatness onto and into others, I need to continue to be poured *into*. You do, too. You can't act like you don't need a greater source of strength.

I am so grateful that I have a wonderful relationship with God. He is my strength. He is my all and all. He blessed me with each gift that I have and display. My friend, I am not attempting to preach to you. I just want you to understand and admit that like a cell phone, we as humans have to realize that we need to plug into a source far greater than ourselves for strength, rejuvenation, and fulfillment. I pour into myself in multiple ways, such as going for nice walks, reading great books, routine exercise, going to the beach, attending church, volunteering, going to conferences, listening to empowering tapes and CDs, and watching inspiring DVDs. When you feel like the world is against you, remember that if you have a relationship with God, everything will be all right. Give back to the most important person you know—yourself!

> Greater is he that is in you, than he that is in the world.
>
> —1 John 4:4

7. Expect to do much of it alone.

Goodness is free, but greatness will cost you! "Cost me what?" you ask. The lonely work! I know so many people who started on the road to their dream but then did a U-turn because they thought that the highway to greatness would be packed full of the same type of people who were on the monorail to mediocrity. Not so! There will be many times when the dream that you are chasing has you working 100 percent by yourself. This is not a bad thing! In fact, this is a great thing. Why? Because you get a chance to learn more about yourself. You get a chance to come face-to-face with you and see what you are really made of when you don't have anyone else around cheering you on. What you do in your secret, private, and personal time—when focusing on your dream—determines the magnitude of your outward reward. Remember these words from a speech by Dr. Stephen Covey: "Private success will always come before public success." Take right now, for example. While writing this chapter, I am sitting in my pajamas, listening to some light mood music, and typing this book. No one is

> We don't stop playing because we grow old; we grow old because we stop playing.[4]
>
> —George Bernard Shaw

around—no kids, no wife, no family, no friends, no co-workers, and no pets. There is nothing but myself, my God, my dream, my destiny, my reasons, my determination, my focus, my greatness, my gifting, my life story, my paradigm, my insight, my foresight, my goals, and my passion for wanting to give my best to you. Come to think of it, I am not that lonely at all. I have a host of friends around me that believe in my success.

> How you think about a problem is more important than the problem itself—so always think positively.[5]
> —Norman Vincent Peale

Guess what? So do you! Now, once this book is published, thousands will come up to me in excitement to get it signed. But nobody was around when I actually typed it all those late nights. Even though I speak to thousands, when it comes to giving birth to new things for my business, much of it must come from within and come during the lonely hours of preparation for an opportunity that does not even exist yet. Wow! That's why you need to expect to do much of the work alone. Unless you have a business partner, which is a great idea in some cases, come to grips with the emotional reality that although people may support you and believe in you, most of those people are not around when you have to actually crank out the work. So the key is to never rely on the public praise of people. Do what you do for you and to benefit others, and let the difference you will make be your company during the alone times.

8. Celebrate yourself often!

Right now, I want you to stop reading this book, go buy some confetti, throw it high in the air in front of you, and walk through your own celebration. That sounds silly, right? Not really, my friend. You see, nobody is going to celebrate you enough for the amount of trouble that you go through in the run of a day. They just won't. That's too much to ask from a teacher, boss, spouse, best friend, or family member. You have to learn to throw your own party. Celebrate YOU! You deserve it. Take yourself to dinner sometimes. Buy yourself something nice, because you have worked for it. If you don't have a special person in your life who does these things for you, treat yourself to massages, manicures, pedicures, and things that celebrate your wellness and esteem. With all the changing, working, negotiating, sacrificing, serving, and creating that you will be doing, it is a must that you pour back into yourself with fun stuff! Laugh a lot. Smile as much as you can. Wave at people who don't know you! Why? Because as Anthony Robbins says, "Your physiology determines your psychology!" In other words, what you do with your body and gestures determines your attitude and mental framework. Celebrate your uniqueness, celebrate your power, celebrate your victories, celebrate the doors that opened for you, celebrate the doors that were closed for you, and most of all, celebrate how blessed you are to have life. Pay close attention to the first persons you call when you get good news. This is an indicator of the key celebrators in your life. Keep these people close to you. They are your own personal cheerleading squad. We all need one. Celebrate the process!

9. Filter your stress often.

Stress is the number-one killer and cause of disease in America. Identify and implement ways you can relieve yourself of stress. You need an outlet for your stress, or it will cause you to become an emotional wreck. People filter stress in different ways. Some read, write, go to the park, walk the dog, make love to their spouse, play a sport, work out, rent a movie, cook, write in a journal, go for a swim, sit in a Jacuzzi, go to a day spa, go shopping, go for a long drive, take a power nap, or go on regular weekend vacations. Whatever method you use, achieve the goal of keeping negative stress at a minimum in your life.

10. Use everything painful for something powerful!

My friend, please get this point. There is a purpose behind your pain. Every hurtful, harmful, painful thing that you go through in life has a major purpose behind it. *There is a life lesson that is fueling every painful situation you encounter.* Allow me to encourage you by telling you to ask God for one simple gift. Ask Him to teach you the life lesson behind every painful situation that happens to you. This goes for the big and small stuff.

Several years ago I was checking my online business bank account, and it was overdrawn by a small but significant amount. I was shocked because as a part of my daily success routine, I check and update all of my online bank accounts. I did not understand what was going on. I balanced my checkbook over again. I called customer service, and I even visited the local bank branch. I had to research back three months to find the error. I found a few small miscalculations on my part and deposited the needed amount to

> There's no scarcity of opportunity to make a living at what you love. There is only a scarcity of resolve to make it happen.[6]
> —Wayne Dyer

clear things up. As I was driving home, I asked, "God, what was I supposed to learn from that?" I felt Him say this back to me: "Well, right now one hundred dollars off when you are earning about one hundred thousand dollars a year seems small, but I want to teach you to be a solid financial steward over your money so that when I bless you to earn one million dollars, you won't miscalculate tens of thousands of dollars!" Wow! God was using something small to teach me an important lesson that I would not want to learn later, because that same lesson learned later would have cost me *much* more!

All pain has a purpose and a push to it. We talked about this in chapter 3, so I won't go back over it, but remember to learn from everything you *grow* through, and also remember that since all pain has some form of push to it, allow the push of pain to take you higher, not pull you down lower.

In conclusion, please know that there is a lot more for you to learn and implement about spiritual and emotional success while transitioning from your job to your dream. My goal here was simply to give you a few TIPS that you could begin to implement right away. Each one of the numbers above could be a book or seminar by itself. So keep learning and keep growing. Your spiritual well-being and your emotional well-being are two of the most important aspects of your self-development as you walk out the gifting and the mission that has been placed on your life. Use these points above, combined with others that you have learned and will learn from other speakers, teachers, lecturers, mentors, preachers, bosses, and advisors, to continue to keep you sharp and focused on fulfilling your destiny and making one of the most powerful transitions you will ever make.

CHAPTER SUMMARY

EIGHT POINTS TO PONDER
DURING YOUR TRANSITION

1. Remember we are all made up of mind, body, and spirit. The greatest of these is our spirit. Nourish and empower your spirit within, and you will achieve anything you can imagine without.

2. Your "I WILL" is more powerful then your "IQ." Your spirit is stronger than your mind. Your mind conceives while the spirit achieves.

3. Remember that you are just like a cell phone. Your spirit needs to be consistently recharged for optimal use. Plug into your greater source. Connect to God, and allow Him to sustain you.

4. Gratitude is a success magnet, and it pulls more of what you are thankful for toward you.

5. Keep growing and contributing. These are the two human needs of the spirit that must be met. Grow more, and give more!

6. Get comfortable with being stretched. Life is no longer easy street for you. This is going to be an excited but diverse journey. Learn to multitask now!

7. Do the lonely work. That's when the real greatness is born. Don't be afraid of the lonely work, because you will be rewarded openly when the time comes.

8. Celebrate the journey often. Filter that stress of yours in exciting and rejuvenating ways, and use the push of pain to teach you and propel you forward and upward.

CHAPTER 10

SOCIAL AND RELATIONAL TIPS

The most important single ingredient in the formula of
success is knowing how to get along with people.[1]
—Theodore Roosevelt

THERE ARE VARIOUS TYPES OF WEALTH. MOST PEOPLE MEASURE WEALTH in terms of financial capital, assets, real estate portfolios, stocks/bonds, and cold hard cash, which we all know is the most prevalent form of wealth. However, I would like to submit to you that there are other forms of wealth and capital. These forms include emotional, spiritual, intellectual, familial, and relational capital. In this chapter, I would like us to focus on the latter of these forms, which makes up the next pillar under the bridge between your job and your dream.

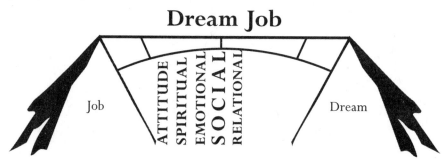

Relational capital is simply how wealthy a person is in terms of their relationships and connections. See, you can have a great deal of money and have a bunch of "*fake*lationships," but over time, you will yearn for "*real*lationships." You will want people who want you for you, not for what you can give them or buy them. It's wonderful to have all forms of wealth operating in your life, where you are rich in spirit, mind, body, soul, money, friends, and family! What a combination, and it's possible! But I would like to say that it is the people in our lives who make life worth living because financial success without loved ones to share it with is very empty. Additionally, success without a successor is really failure. When it comes to relationships overall, the people in your life can either be your greatest asset or your greatest liability! So during your transition from job living to dream living, it is absolutely critical that you know how to conduct yourself in public and how to connect with the right people and disconnect from the wrong ones.

SOCIAL AND RELATIONAL TIPS
FOR SUCCESS IN YOUR DREAM JOB

1. Be quiet! (Don't tell everyone.)

Audiences love this one. You know, sometimes we are our worst enemy because we advertise our plans to the wrong people! We prematurely share our most intimate goals and dreams with individuals whom we want to believe in us, but in truth these people don't. The wrong people are those who are incapable of helping us live our dream. During your transition, you must know that some people will support you, but many will think you are crazy. So although you are excited about your dream and you want others to be excited, too, do me a favor and just be quiet! As you begin to make the transition from your job to your dream, don't market it. Only tell your mentors and close positive friends and family. That's it! The only people who need to know about your dreams are those who are able and willing to help you get them. The *only* people who need to know about your dreams are those who are able and willing to help you get them. The *only* people who need to know about your dreams are those who are able and willing to help you get them. That is not a typo! Repetition is the mother of skill. You must get this point. Don't tell everyone about your plans, especially people you work with, because if it gets out that you have greater interests beyond the job, you can find yourself getting fired or let go much earlier then you anticipated. Tell only those whose wisdom and resources will help your journey.

2. Get business cards and Web presence.

I got my first business card at the age of fourteen. It was simple, but it taught me how to present myself professionally and leave an impression on everyone I met. By the way, your new business cards need to advertise your new dream— not your dream job! Remember the dream job is a temporary place, so don't overadvertise it. Advertise where you are going, not where you are. Focus on your future. When you are out and about town, only present your dream business card to people. When someone comes up to you and asks you what you do and where you work, always present your dream first; then if it comes up, tell them you have a job doing such and such. The only time you need to market the business cards of your job is when you are at a function that is related to your job or a function that your job is paying you to attend. You will know when to use what card, but don't mix them up. I have seen many people try to promote their job and the dream on the same card, although they are two totally different things. You don't want to do this; please keep them separate! Additionally, get some Web presence. With today's viral global Internet world and society, it's easier than ever to get yourself exposure on the Web. Back in the day, it was costly but necessary to get a Web site built for your brand-new business. Now with network marketing companies providing their associates very nice Web sites for very little each month, and with the advent of MySpace, Facebook, and other networking and online community Web sites, it's easier than ever to build a single page Web site that promotes what you do! Visit www.novaltravel.com to see what I mean.

> It's not about who you know; it's who knows you![2]
>
> —Jeffrey Gitomer

I know you're probably saying, "Del, you just told me to be quiet. Wouldn't business cards and community Web sites announce my business to people?" You need to develop a client base for your dream. A client base is a listing of potential people who can benefit from your services and become customers. Business cards let people know that you are serious. They communicate a level of professionalism and pursuit after your dream. They also remind you of the problem that you solve for others. Sharing a business card and a Web site is one thing; sharing a business plan and your transition strategies is totally different. Be smart! My rule of thumb is this: I keep my dream moves very quiet until they are almost complete or ready to be revealed, and then I reveal what I have been working on. Many people think that I created it overnight because I did not mention it, but in truth, I had been working on it for many years or months by the time most people find out. You should do the same. Protect your dreams!

3. Network like it's going out of style!

Les Brown, a good friend and mentor of mine, says that you should network as if you haven't met 50 percent of the people who are going to be responsible for helping you achieve your dream. That means you need to network! All you need is to connect with the right person, at the right place, at the right time, with the right product or service, and it's all over! Once you get your business cards (by the way, Vistaprint.com is an excellent and inexpensive starting point), take them with you at all times. Everyone you meet needs to have a good impression of you left behind so that they can contact you at a future date (when they are ready for you to solve a problem for them). Put yourself in the right place at the right time. Open up your local newspaper and look in the career section or the local happenings section, and you will see tons of networking opportunities in your local area that you can attend. Many of these events are free! Also, I recommend joining a networking or leads group because once you do this, you will now have a team of business professionals that will help you to market and advertise your dreams. Speed networking events are another great way to get more people to know about you. Joining a service organization like Rotary, Kiwanis, Toastmasters, or any of the like are great additional ways to develop yourself and make a difference at the same time. We talked in chapter 7 about conferences and conventions. These are great ways to network on the national and international levels because many times people come from around the country and around the world to attend certain major conferences. Take tons of cards, build relationships, and, the biggest key to all networking . . . follow up!

> Rich relationships lead to much more than money! They lead to success, fulfillment, and wealth![3]
>
> —Jeffrey Gitomer

4. Treat everyone you meet with respect.

You don't know whom the person you just ignored or treated badly knows. You don't know who the person in traffic you just flicked off is. Just because people are dressed casually or you see them in casual situations does not mean they are not important. This reminds me of an incident that happened in the grocery store recently. I saw a man walking opposite me down the bread aisle.

It was my intention not to speak, but he actually spoke first, so I spoke and was friendly. Thank God I was, because although I did not remember him, he remembered me. He was in an audience that I had spoken to over two years prior. He approached me in the checkout line, and we had a great conversation. Had I treated him as I was a little tempted to at first (just being honest—that was a very challenging day), I would have potentially messed up the strong impression he had of me from the event he had attended. Treat everyone in public and private with the same love and respect you would want. Again, you never know who someone knows, so don't underestimate anyone!

5. Change your friends and inner circle.

This is huge before, during, and after your transition. Don't use the word *friends* as an all-encompassing term to describe all of the people in your life. Not everyone in your life is there to empower you. I would be willing to bet that a third of the people you call friends may not be your true friends at all.

> **If you want to soar like an eagle, you can't hang out with turkeys!**
>
> **—Author Unknown**

So change your friends. The peers you surround yourself with should be people who add to your life. You see, there are four types of people in this world: those who add, multiply, subtract, or divide. Keep those who add joy, multiply your opportunities, subtract worry, and divide your enemies. Remove those who add drama, multiply your past mistakes, subtract your peace, and divide your focus. It's that simple. And notice what I said: *change* your friends. I didn't say discard. What I mean is that we all have a human need for connection and significance, so it's not smart to just get rid of all of your friends; rather, replace them! For every negative person you remove from your life, replace them with two positive ones. Your inner circle needs to be a tight mesh of positive peers who believe in you 100 percent. They are out there, but you have to find them and build those relationships one person at a time.

6. Develop a mastermind group.

Napoleon Hill talks about this principle in his book *Think and Grow Rich.*[4] Dr. Mike Murdock says, "There are two ways to get wisdom: mistakes and mentors."[5] I have had my share of mistakes, and I prefer mentors. A mastermind group is a group of people whose minds and intellect you value. A mastermind group will help you cut your learning curve in half. These people will protect you, look out for you, create opportunities for you, advise you, counsel you, invest in you, sharpen you, and build you. All of your major decisions in life need to be run through your mastermind group. You should meet with them monthly and consult with them weekly; always seek to learn from them as they learn from you. I have mastermind groups for speaking, music, business, fatherhood, marriage, and overall personal development.

7. Surround yourself with the three *M*s—mentors, mates, and mentees

There should be three types of people in your life at all times. I teach this all across the country, and every audience really enjoys and benefits from it.

1. Mentor. I have talked extensively about mentorship in this chapter because it's so critical. Most of the self-made millionaires in this country have many things in common. One of those things is that they all had financial mentors in their lives. Mentors are learning-curve cutters! They help you get to your goal quicker and with less heartache than they had. You should always be reaching up to their level. Critical point: Don't pursue a mentor for what they have earned (degrees, houses, cars, clothes, and the like). Pursue a mentor for what they have learned (wisdom, insight, life lessons, character, and integrity). So the first person you should have in your life is someone who is above you. Dr. Mike Murdock's book *The Law of Recognition* will teach you a lot about how to recognize mentors in your life.[6] Talk with your mentor at least once a month with major updates, progress, and setbacks that you have encountered. Many times, these people will be very busy, so use their time wisely.

2. Mate. This is like a running mate. This is someone who is at a similar age and stage as you are in life. Why choose someone like this? Because you want someone you can bounce ideas off of. You want someone with whom you can experience similar successes and failures. You will rise up the success ladder together with this person, and that makes the journey, which is a huge part of your success, more enjoyable and adventurous.

3. Mentee. This is someone whom you are pouring into. This is someone whose learning curve you are cutting. This is someone who looks to you as their mentor. Now the tables are turned, and you are not focused on getting—you are focused on giving. Mentees are great because they force you to review the totality of your life and squeeze out some nuggets of truth that can help them avoid the many mistakes and pitfalls that you encountered. You need someone into whom you can dump your life lessons so that what you go through will not be in vain; it will have been of some benefit to someone else as well as yourself.

If you will keep these three types of people around you and inside your life at all times, you will have a powerful team of people who will help you make a successful transition and elevation from one level of greatness to another.

8. Get a coach *now*!

"Del, what's the difference between a mentor and a coach?" you may be asking. In my opinion, a mentor is someone whose time and wisdom is so valuable that you would be almost disrespecting them by bothering them daily with your issues. A coach, on the other hand, is someone whom you hire to get down in the trenches with you. They see your pitfalls, valleys, successes, downtimes, and are there to coach you through them. They correct you, help discipline you, and encourage you on a weekly basis. Perfect example: Les Brown and Willie Jolley are two of my mentors in the speaking industry. I have all of their contact information, and I can call them anytime—day or night. However, I only communicate with them monthly. Why? Because they are extremely busy people. Hogging their time on a weekly basis would be very rude of me. I have national speaker friends and colleagues whom I talk with weekly and sometimes daily, and we coach each other. We sharpen each other on products, marketing, Web sites, and bookings. These are my coaches, and I am their coach. I have a fitness coach, a financial coach, a product development coach, a parenting coach, a marriage enrichment coach, and the list goes on. I purposely seek out coaches in all areas of my life so that I can operate in wisdom in all of my decisions and dealings. The personal and business coaching industry is so huge right

> Treasure your relationships; they are worth more than your possessions.
>
> —Anthony J. D'Angelo

now. So if you feel you need a coach in any area of your life, go get one. You can hire a coach on a short-term or long-term basis, but the key is to get the help you need to become better. Does having mentors and coaches exempt you from making mistakes and bad decisions? No. But they do greatly decrease your failures and increase your successes. Surround yourself with people who have been there and done that, so that you can go there and do that!

9. Maintain a contact management system.

It's one thing to master your time; it's another to master your relationships. Jeffrey Gitomer has a great book called *Little Black Book of Connections*.[7] I highly recommend that you read that book and glean from it the skills you need to build and maintain solid relationships. Simply put, you need a way of managing all the people you meet, the business cards you collect, the contacts you make, and the relationships you build. In the next chapter, we will talk about time-mastery tools and devices. You should use these same devices to maintain your relationships. However, I would like to add that it's really important to stay in contact with important people in your life. Celebrate them, call them on their birthday, support events and causes that they believe in, buy them a copy of a book you know they want to read, and so on. Celebrate those that you value in your life.

CHAPTER SUMMARY

EIGHT POINTS TO PONDER
DURING YOUR TRANSITION

1. Remember the five forms of wealth: spiritual, financial, emotional, intellectual, familial, and relational capital.

2. Financial success without someone to share it with is empty, and success without a successor is really failure.

3. Keep quiet about your dreams until they are almost fully realized. The only people that need to know about your dreams are those who can help you achieve them.

4. In social settings, always promote your dream over your current job. Talk about where you are going, not so much where you are today. Use business cards and the power of the Internet to promote your dreams to people and stay connected.

5. Protect your dreams just as a mother protects her newborn! Enough said.

6. Remember to network as if you haven't yet met 50 percent of the people responsible for helping you with your dreams. Think of all the relational capital that is waiting at networking functions for you to acquire.

7. Remember the four types of people in the world: those whom add, subtract, multiply, and divide. Make those who do these four things positive and key parts of your inner circle.

8. The greatest assets to your life and dreams are mastermind groups, mentors, mates, mentees, and coaches. Utilize them all to make you better!

CHAPTER 11

TIME MASTERY TIPS

Stop asking your time where it went, and start
telling your time where to go.

—Scott Thomas

WE HEAR IT ALL THE TIME. PEOPLE SAY, "OH MAN, WHERE DID THE time go?" or "I wish I had more time in the day" or "I just wish that I could buy more hours in the day." And while hoping and wishing for these things to happen is fine and dandy, it is neither effective nor efficient, because in truth, time is the great equalizer. People have different income levels and different socioeconomic statuses; however, when it comes to the amount of time we have, we are all in the same boat. Money can buy almost everything, but it can't buy more hours in the day, more days in the month, or more months in the year. When was the last time you saw an eighteen-month year for sale on eBay to the highest bidder? Time is the greatest asset that you have. Today is a gift; that's why it's called the present. Your today creates your tomorrow. Tomorrow can change based on your actions or inactions today. You can't get back yesterday, so stop trying. Live in the only thing you have direct control over, and that's right now!

As it relates to time, your mind performs three functions daily. It replays the past, plays the present, or preplays the future. Replaying the past is called memory. Playing the present is called process. Preplaying the future is called vision. We just talked earlier about the power of leading your life and your dream with a vision. Time is another pillar to lean on during your transition from your job to your dream and beyond; here are a few TIPS for mastering it.

Dream Job

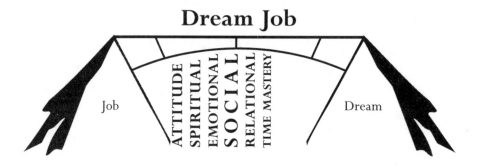

Time Mastery TIPS for Success in Your Dream Job

1. Purchase a planner/organizer, and actually use it.

I know that this sounds simple, but you would be absolutely amazed at the number of people who want to manage their time better yet have no way of keeping track of it. Determine what type of person you are. Do you like to handwrite your daily activities, tasks, and appointments? If so, then get a paper planner like a Franklin Covey or a Day-Timer. If you are much more technology oriented, you probably want to invest in a Palm, pocket PC, PDA/phone, iPhone, Treo, Blackberry, or some other type of PDA (personal digital assistant).

Now, once you get an organizer, make sure you use it. I know many people who have purchased equipment to help manage their time, but the planners are sitting at home in the same box that they were purchased in. Use the stuff! Work toward putting all of your appointments, contacts, tasks, and lists in one place. "Well, Del," you may be saying, "I would love to do that, but I am afraid that if I lose it, I will lose everything. What do I do?" If you have this concern, I would recommend leaning more toward the technology-oriented side of time and life organization. Electronic databases like Outlook, Goldmine, and ACT! allow you to make master copies of your information on your hard drive, jump drive, CD, or DVD while also allowing you to synchronize that same information with your PDA or phone. Invest in a device that pertains to the chronological details of your life. How can you manage and

> Until you value yourself, you will not value your time. Until you value your time you will not do anything with it.
>
> —M. Scott Peck

master what you can't see? Trying to master your time without a paper or electronic device is just like trying to manage your money without bank statements or online account access. It's pointless. So invest in a time mastery product that you will use, and use it faithfully.

2. Write a task list each morning, and work from it.

This is a habit that I developed and have operated in for many years now. When I get up each morning, I make a simple list of what I want accomplish in the day. This includes people I need to call, e-mail, write, or meet; things I need to mail or purchase; appointments I need to schedule; and presentations I need to prepare. I work from this list and strike through each item as I complete it. Lists allow you to build momentum. In addition to building momentum, they allow you to take inventory of how you are investing your time and the benefits you can expect from your labor. Trust me, I have not always been this way.

When I was younger, I wasted enough time for several people. If you aim at nothing in your day, you will hit your target every time. Focus your time and energy each day by starting your morning with a task list. You will be amazed how many things you will accomplish each day. Zig Ziglar said something on a CD I was listening to many years ago. He said, "Isn't it amazing how productive we are the day before we go on vacation?"[1] Basically his point was that if we could approach each day with the tenacity, fervor, detail, organization, and enthusiasm that we put forth on the day before we go on vacation, we all would be one hundred times more successful than we could ever imagine. The thing about time is that it's going to pass whether you are productive or not, so you might as well maximize it! It's the most valuable resource and asset you have!

> **Time invested is always more fruitful than time spent. So stop spending time, and start investing it. You will be amazed at the returns!**
> **—Delatorro L. McNeal II**

3. Develop a daily routine.

Dr. John Maxwell and Dr. Mike Murdock both teach that "the secret of your success is found in your daily routine/agenda."[2] Dr. Maxwell believes so much in the power of each day that he wrote a book called *Today Matters*, which I highly recommend.[3] In this book, he speaks about the importance of approaching each day with a routine or an agenda already in mind. Now a daily routine and a daily list of tasks are two totally different things. Working from a task list each day allows you to see the things that are important that specific day and build momentum and a sense of accomplishment by checking off the items as you complete them. Additionally, doing this keeps you from dropping the ball on important tasks. However, tasks change daily, so what's important today may be minor tomorrow. A daily routine, on the other hand, is a more permanent and consistent way of living your daily life, which enables you to embed within your day small activities (habits) that are nugget-size representations of your short-term and long-term goals. The reason why both of these incredible men believe in the power of each day so much is because within each day lie the keys that create success or failure. Dissecting your daily routine will reveal the hidden actions or inactions that are pushing you toward success or pulling your toward failure. Activities in your daily routine could include things like the following:

> Lost wealth may be replaced by industry, lost knowledge by study, lost health by temperance or medicine, but lost time is gone forever.[4]
>
> —Samuel Smiles

- Drinking eight glasses of water
- Reading over your goals as you brush your teeth
- Listening to a motivational CD while driving to work
- Taking a walk around your neighborhood right after work
- Reading a special affirmation you keep in your purse or wallet
- Saying your prayers before you go to bed
- And many more

The point is, the things that make up your to-do list are tasks, but the things that make up your daily routine are habits, and healthy success habits are what create massive success on a variety of levels. The truth is, you already have a daily routine. Each day almost by default you do certain things automatically without even thinking. Well, once you ingrain healthy habits into each day, habits that you do almost as easily as blinking your eyes, your days will begin to reward you greatly. To master your life, you don't have to master your years, months, or weeks. Just master each day to the best of your ability.

Living your life from a daily routine does not mean that you have do the same boring things day in and day out. You can always spice up your life with spontaneous activities, dates, outings, and fun events that keep life exhilarating! Time mastery is not about making you a schedule nerd but rather someone who values and appreciates the blessing of life and does not waste any of it on negativity.

4. Invest three lunch breaks per week in your dream.

This is one of the most powerful principles that you can execute while in transition between your job and your dream. People tell me all the time that the number one thing that keeps them from building their dream while on the job is *time*—or a lack thereof. I always encourage people who have busy work schedules to do one simple thing: maximize your lunch breaks. Instead of going out with co-workers, eat your lunch at your desk and research on the Internet, take a trip to a store, visit a mentor, or do something—anything—that will feed your dream! It's absolutely critical that you seize the opportunities that your lunch breaks provide. Whatever your dream is, water it with the time you have each day during your lunch hour. When I was transi-

> The distance between the first floor and the second floor is great, but the steps in between are very small. It's little action done consistently that will lead you to your destiny.
> —Delatorro L. McNeal II

tioning from USF to my speaking dream, my co-workers knew that they could only count on me to attend lunch with them maybe one day a week. The rest of those days on my lunch breaks I would go away and read, research, study, practice, or do an actual speaking engagement. Many times during lunch I would go from campus to a hotel across the street, speak for thirty minutes, and come back to my job without skipping a beat. But it took great time mastery and management to pull it off. Think about it: one hour a day equals five hours a week, which is twenty to twenty-five hours per month that you can be building your dream during the days you have at work without being unfaithful to your job. I challenge you to seize the time that you have that you are not paid for. Your drive to work is not paid for, and neither is your drive from home. Don't spend time worrying about work when you are *not* on the clock. Invest that time in your dream!

5. Invest one extra hour per day into your dream.

You have twenty-four hours in a day. That's eight hours to work, eight hours to sleep, and eight hours for yourself. I want you to not only seize your lunch breaks, but also invest one of those eight extra hours that you have into your dream. TiVo your sitcoms and watch them as you go to bed so you can laugh on your way to sleep. But don't let your television shows run your time. Record them, and watch them on your time! The only difference between the ordinary and the extraordinary is a little extra. So I double dog dare you to squeeze an extra hour out of each day that you are blessed to live. Remember what I told you earlier: whatever you water is what will grow. During my transition, my normal day was eight to five with an hour in the middle that I used

Time flies. It's up to you to be the navigator.[5]

—**Robert Orben**

to work on my dream. Then after work, I would come home and work from about 6:30 to 9:00 p.m. on my dream, which because I loved it didn't even feel like work. When you do what you are passionate about, the time flies by and your labor toward your dream feels more like a hobby that you do to unwind and recharge from a long day at work.

6. Understand the three phases of your time.

During your transition, I recommend that you adopt three phases of thinking about your time:

1. Job time: the time you invest while working your job or soon-to-be dream job. It's the time invested in your bridge from where you are to where you want to be.

2. Dream time: the time you invest specially working on your dream. That could be reading, writing, studying, learning, taking classes, researching online, attending conferences, networking, doing internships, watching a TV show that relates to your dream, and so on.

3. Me time: sleep, rest, relaxation, recreational time, family time, spiritual empowerment time, yoga time, or whatever you feel you want or need to do to recharge "me."

So with these three mental tracks, if you are not on the job, you are either enjoying me time or you're investing in dream time. It's that simple!

7. Know when it's your time to move on.

It is going to be very important that you discern and be sensitive to when it's your time to do certain things, make certain moves, and step away as you continue to transition from your job to your dream. Timing is very important. A bridge, which essentially is what the dream job is, is meant to get you from one side to another. But you're not supposed to camp out on the bridge! And just as you need to know when to enter, you need to know when to exit, too. When you exit, you want to exit at the top of your game in the dream job. You want to leave on good terms, because people remember your exit more so than your entrance. Although after working at USF for two years and making great money in speaking at the same time, I was still a little nervous and scared when I turned in my letter of resignation and two weeks notice. On my very last day, I cried all the way from my office to my car and most of the way home, because I knew that from then on, I was completely in God's hands for the ultimate provision of my business, goals, and dreams. There was no more safety net called a job or a salary that would catch me if I fell. I was going to work as if it all depended on me and pray as if it all depended on God. My point is that you have to know when it's your time to go, and when that time comes, don't just fly . . . soar!

> **Your greatest resource is your time.**
> —Brian Tracy

> To every thing there is a season, and a time to every purpose under the heaven:
> A time to be born, and a time to die; a time to plant, and a time to pluck up that which is planted;
> A time to kill, and a time to heal; a time to break down, and a time to build up;
> A time to weep, and a time to laugh; a time to mourn, and a time to dance;
> A time to cast away stones, and a time to gather stones together; a time to embrace, and a time to refrain from embracing;
> A time to get, and a time to lose; a time to keep, and a time to cast away;
> A time to rend, and a time to sew; a time to keep silence, and a time to speak;
> A time to love, and a time to hate, a time of war, and a time of peace.
> —Ecclesiastes 3:1–8

CHAPTER SUMMARY

EIGHT POINTS TO PONDER
DURING YOUR TRANSITION

1. Today is a gift; that's why they call it the present. Don't live in yesterday; it's gone. Don't live in tomorrow; it's not here yet.

2. Get a vision for your future, and create it today. Live in the now!

3. Time invested is more fruitful than time spent, so stop spending time and start investing time. Your will be amazed at the return.

4. You already have a daily routine. Dissect it and reconstruct it so it can create success for you automatically.

5. Don't stress about work when you are not on the clock. Invest that time in your dreams.

6. Spend lunch breaks and one extra hour per day investing in your dream, and you will transition much faster than you anticipate.

7. Remember, your mind should process time in three ways: job time, dream time, and me time!

8. Know when it's your time to go, and when your time comes, don't just fly . . . soar!

CHAPTER 12

FINANCIAL AND ENTREPRENEURIAL TIPS

I had to make my own living and my own opportunity!
But I made it! Don't sit down and wait for the
opportunities to come. Get up and make them![1]
—Madam C. J. Walker

W ELCOME TO THE LAST OF THE TIPS CHAPTERS AND NUMERICALLY the last chapter of the book. I am so incredibly proud of you for coming this far in your amazing journey of discovery as you walk out the steps needed to transition from your job to your dream. The topics of money and business are so huge that colleges and universities offer bachelor's and master's programs in these fields and still don't exhaust the depth of content that lies beneath each one. So, my goal in this chapter is not to be deep but rather to be practical and tactical. I want to give you some simple suggestions and another pillar that I used on my way to my dream. I have helped others utilize this pillar in order to make it across the bridge from their job to the dream.

Dream Job

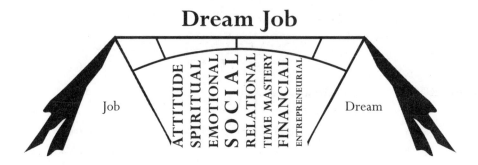

I love the quote that opened this chapter because it is so true. In money and business, you can't wait for things to just come to you; you have to go after what you want. There's no free lunch, and there are no handouts in money and business. You will have to work for your dream. If living your dreams were easy, everyone would be doing it. Robert Kiyosaki says something I like and use in my keynotes and seminars: there are three ways to get anything you want in life:

- Step one: Identify the thing you want.
- Step two: Identify the price that the thing you want costs.
- Step three: Pay the price.[2]

Madam C. J. Walker, America's first black female millionaire, did exactly that. She paid the price to be an entrepreneur and an innovator in the field of education. Her legacy still lives on today. The point is simple: there is a significant price that you will have to pay to get across the bridge, but the reward that awaits you on the other side is wonderful. Enjoy the journey, but be proactive about taking control of your life and making the most of every opportunity that comes your way. The interesting thing is that if you don't cross the bridge, you will pay an even heftier price—the price of regret for not making the transition. So go ahead; pay the price so you can live your dreams. The TIPS that follow are very specific to your transition process. Once you get from your job to your dream job and then into your dream, you will need financial strategies more advanced than these, but these will serve as foundational material upon which you can build. Keep in mind, however, that although some of these concepts are simple to grasp, they may take several months, if not several years, to fully implement into your life.

> Passion is energy. Feel the power that comes from focusing on what excites you.[3]
>
> —Oprah Winfrey

FINANCIAL AND ENTREPRENEURIAL TIPS FOR SUCCESS IN YOUR DREAM JOB

1. Use your dream job to build a solid financial foundation for your dream.

Trust me, you want as little financial pressure resting on your dream as possible. You don't want to quit a job and rely solely on your dream to dig you out of credit card debt, personal debt, student loan debt, and a lot of consumer debt. Your dream needs your mind to be free for creativity and innovation, so you want to put less stress on your dream, especially in the beginning, by using your dream job and your dream to pay off a large percentage of your unsecured debts. Remember to treat your dream like it's a newborn baby. Give it the time, love, attention, devotion, nourishment, care, protection, and provision that you give a child, and watch it grow like a child grows into an adult. Now, once your dream gets older and stronger and can handle more stress and pressure, then you can put certain financial responsibilities and liabilities on it. But starting off, use your job and the income from your blossoming dream to help fund your debt-freedom program. Statistics say that it takes the average small business two to three years to turn its first real profit, so don't choke your dream by putting too much on it too soon.

> Empty pockets never held anyone back. Only empty heads and empty hearts can do that.[6]
> —Norman Vincent Peale

Many times with new businesses, banks and lending institutions want the business debt to be personally guaranteed by the owner of that business, so you need your personal credit to be good—not great and not perfect, but at least somewhat good—so that your business stands a better chance of getting the up-front capital it needs to survive and grow.

While you are getting your debts paid down or off, start saving for your dream. Set some money aside automatically out of your check if you can, or set up an automatic bill payment to your dream account from your job account that you don't have to touch. Even if it's something small, at least it's something. Leave willpower and discipline out of it. The government found a way to pay themselves first and automatically, and you should do the same. Every great financial expert talks about the importance of paying yourself first. Many of them mean in terms of paying into your retirement accounts, but that money can go into retirement accounts, dream business accounts, personal accounts, or what have you as long as you keep yourself a top priority. So really work that dream job, and do it for as long as you need to so that you can make a successful and lasting transition from your job to your dream. If you recall my first year in the dream job at USF, my speaking dream earned more income that year than my job. Many of my friends at that point thought that I should have left, but I could not. I needed that second year for a very powerful reason.

2. Think multiple streams of income.

Robert Allen is one of the kings of this concept, and his book *Multiple Streams of Income* will transform your life.[5] The reason I worked a second year at USF is because I wanted to maintain both streams of income for as long as I could without damaging either one. After my speaking dream hit six figures, I was speaking too much to be part-time, and that's when I left. I mentioned this to you earlier in the book: for almost all of my working life, I have had multiple streams of income flowing into my life. Some of it was passive residual income and some of it was active residual income, but the good thing was that all of it was multiple! This is one the most powerful strategies of successful businesspeople and wealthy people. *Forbes* magazine reported that the top twenty wealthiest people in the world make their money from over nine different industries.[7] So as you begin your transition, it's time you really think of ways you can bring more money into your life, which simply means that you need to find more problems to solve for others and solve them in more ways! Remember, if you are like most, your money is going out of your accounts in many ways (bills), so your money needs to be coming in, in many ways (checks) also.

> If a person gets his attitude toward money straight, it will help straighten out almost any other area of his life.[7]
>
> —Billy Graham

3. Hire a certified financial planner (CFP) as soon as possible.

A good financial planner will conduct a financial needs assessment or analysis on you and your business to help you determine your debt-freedom date as well as the types of funds you will need to launch your dreams and sustain them. Additionally, a good CFP can educate you in terms of the different investment vehicles you can use to put money aside in your business that is tax deferred. They can talk with you about the advantages and disadvantages of small business development loans if you are considering that option. One of the biggest things that your CFP will do is help you determine how long you will need to stay in your dream job in order to be in good enough financial shape to step out into your dream full-time. Trust me, you don't want to step out there on emotion alone. It will bankrupt you quickly. I have seen it happen too many times. Be smart, and find a CFP you trust. Be financially naked with them. Show them your personal and business budget, go over your credit report, disclose all of your debt, bring a copy of your goals for the next three to five years, and allow them to get into the details of your financial life so they can help you create an effective blueprint. Each person's transition story and timeline is different, so you need customized help from professionals. Don't try to make these decisions alone. Invest in good advice!

> What material success does is provide you with the ability to concentrate on other things that really matter. And that is being able to make a difference, not only in your own life, but in other people's lives.[8]
> —Oprah Winfry

4. Use your dream job to finance major purchases.

If you know that you want to buy a home, get a newer car, or make some other major investment, take those steps with the security and backing of your dream job. Most financial institutions would trust the name of an established employer much faster than they would your new business venture. You will have much fewer headaches this way. When my wife and I were transitioning, we bought our first home, upgraded our cars, and did a few other things under the name, income, and credibility of our jobs, not our dreams. In many cases, your dream income does not even count as real income until you have two years of tax returns to validate it. Lenders and banks like to see consistency with your income, so use your dream job to get you qualified for most of the major purchases you want to make while in transition. I strongly recommend home ownership because, when done the right way, buying a house in a market that is increasing in value will add to your overall net worth, and that appreciating house value can help your business later on down the road. I shifted from renting to owning during the same time I was transitioning from jobbing to dreaming! You can do the same.

5. Establish bank accounts and credit in the name of your dream as soon as possible.

Give your dream or your business an identity. Treat it as a person separate from yourself. Take all the official steps necessary to incorporate, obtain tax IDs, and establish credit in the name of your venture so that people and financial institutions will begin to take it seriously. Put all of these things in place for your dream while you are still working in your dream job! There are many great banks and credit unions that have wonderful plans for new and developing businesses and entrepreneurs. Some offer free checking, savings, and other discounts and perks for business owners.

> Money is a good servant but a bad master.
>
> —French Saying

In the previous tip, I talked about home ownership and the benefits of it. Many banks will offer you home equity lines of credit on the equity you have in your home to help get your business started. So for example, let's say that you buy a house while you're working your dream job as I did. You live in it for a year, and when you get it appraised, you learn that your home has increased in value by thirty thousand dollars. Well, you can go into your bank or credit union and apply for a home equity line of credit against that thirty thousand dollars and use that money to build, grow, or expand your business. Find small-business-friendly banks and/or credit unions that you trust, and try to develop a longstanding relationship with them. Your local small-business development center should be very helpful with this. Over time you will see the many benefits of it.

6. Work with a bookkeeper, CPA, and payroll specialist.

These professionals will keep you in line with Uncle Sam and also teach you valuable ways to go about operating your business or functioning in your dream so that it is financially beneficial for you. Trust me, the money they will save you far outweighs the fees they charge to work with you. Do your homework, and find people who have your heartbeat and believe in what you are doing. Ultimately, you will become very financially naked with your CPA as well. You will probably have a similar relationship with them that you have with your CFP. And being financially naked to professionals who can help you and heal you is a wonderful thing. I think that most people mess up because they are not transparent enough with their finances. It's amazing to me how easily we take off our clothes and get naked, or close to it, for doctors who look after our health, but we cover up and hide ourselves from those who seek to look after our wealth! Think about it. Being naked in either way is a very private matter but a very necessary one if we are going to be healthy in our bodies and in our bank accounts. The goal here is to put a quality team of experts all around you and your dream, because your dreams can only grow to the extent of the wisdom that is around them.

7. Think big, start small, and scale fast.

Who wants to be a thousandaire? That's the real million-dollar question! I bring this up for a very powerful reason. In today's game-show and get-rich-quick society, everyone wants to get "there" but they don't want to go through the process. They try to rush the process or somehow get around it by trying the latest and greatest thing. The purpose of this tip is to encourage you that once you set yourself in a direction to go after your dreams, don't let other people, other ventures, other businesses, and other interests sidetrack you from focusing on what you really want. Most people in today's society are just like a cat. Dangle this in front of them and they go left; dangle that in front

> I never perfected an invention that I did not think about in terms of the service it might give others.... I find out what the world needs, then I proceed to invent.[9]
> —Thomas Edison

of them and they go right. Meanwhile, nothing gets accomplished toward what they really want. Only you really know what you really want. Other people may passionately and enthusiastically try to present to you what they want you to want, but ultimately only you can decide that. However, once you decide that— and based on the work you had to do in previous chapters, you already have decided—don't lose that focus. It's cool to have other interests and talents that you develop on the side, but keep the main thing the main thing. Business opportunities are great; however, the wrong ones at the wrong time equal nothing more than distraction in your life.

With that said, once you know what you really want, think big (in terms of billions and trillions of dollars), but then I want you to start small (with something you can manage effectively), and then scale fast (meaning to make consistent, daily progress). How do you climb a ladder? One rung at a time. The same is true of your dreams. Everyone wants to be a millionaire and a billionaire, but it takes being a hundredaire first, then a thousandaire, then a ten thousandaire, then a hundred thousandaire, to become a millionaire. Most people don't go from making thirty thousand dollars a year to millionaire status overnight. Most people have to evolve into their wealth, and so should you. Studies show that those who get it overnight lose it almost twice as fast. But those who grow their wealth, those who think big, start small, and scale fast, can duplicate their success time and time again! They can make money, lose it, and make it again, and they can bounce back from any financial or entrepreneurial failure because the secret is in their way of thinking!

8. Consider a network marketing organization.

Networking marketing (NM), or relationship marketing as it is also called, is a wonderful way for you to take the steps toward entrepreneurship with low risk yet with the potential for high reward. NM organizations provide a variety of powerful benefits to people of all walks of life, but especially those who are tired of the nine-to-five grind and want to transition to a life of freedom and abundance. According the Paul Zane Pilzer, a significant percentage of the world's next millionaires will be people who build NM businesses from the comfort of their own homes. Many NM organizations take advantage of a couple major market shifts, the first being the trend of home-based businesses. Just like Michael Gerber talked about, we are in the age of the entrepreneur, and in this age, people are finding more and more innovative ways to work from home and build entrepreneurial empires, while still being able to invest quality time with family. The second major shift that many NM organizations are leveraging hard is the Internet. As we said earlier, the World Wide Web is not going anywhere anytime soon. In fact, many economic and technological experts are saying that we are just now starting to see the power of the Internet. Additionally, with the advent of VoIP (voice-over-Internet protocol), complex cellular technology, Bluetooth, and a host of other technologies, the virtual office is becoming the new norm.

> Business opportunities are like buses; there's always another one coming.[10]
>
> —Richard Branson

Most solid NM organizations have powerful and seamless distribution models and very attractive compensation plans. One of the biggest benefits is that almost all NM organizations strongly promote the magic of working the business part-time. Mentoring, coaching, training, and shadowing are huge social and educational components and methodologies present in most NM organizations, which allow new people to gain instant access to successful veterans in the company. You can typically meet in person the people at the top of an NM organization just by going to one or two conferences, whereas in a standard corporation you could work at a place for twenty years and never meet the founders or CEO. Another major benefit to the NM organization model is that of leverage. Remember in chapter 9 when I was telling you about doing the lonely work? Well, in most NM organizations you are in business for yourself but not by yourself. Your sponsor typically surrounds you with people who are there to help you succeed. Therefore, you get leverage from the team standpoint, and you get leverage from your down line. Instead of the traditional work model that says that your results and income are predicated on getting 100 percent of one person's effort (your own), in an NM organization, because of your down line, you could potentially get 1 percent of effort from 100 percent of the people, based on the size of the organization you build.

> Wealth is the product of man's capacity to think.[11]
>
> —Ayn Rand

Now as with anything, there are great NM organizations and there are not-so-great ones. My advice is to check a few out and see if you find a product that you believe in and would like to market through your network. Because all you're doing is marketing through your network with minimal overhead and rather rapid returns, a solid NM organization is a great way to add another income stream to your life. Additionally, it's a great way to test your wings to see if you really have what it takes to be a trailblazing entrepreneur in your own ventures.

Visit my Web site at www.DelMcNeal.com to learn about several NM options that may be of interest to you.

9. Continue your learning.

This is one of the biggest things you can do. Keep learning by not only reading great books but also by putting the right people and groups around you to continue to nourish and empower your dreams. Pay for mentorship and coaching if that's what it takes to get around the financial and entrepreneurial greatness that you need to get to your next level. Attend at least two major conferences per year within your specific industry. Shadow the people who do now what you want to do, and see if it's really for you. Study under great entrepreneurs, and take their classes, courses, seminars, and workshops. Don't worry or stress about money. Allow it to flow into your life by being the right type of person and by providing a service to others of great value. Remember that your dream solves a problem for someone. Solve their problem effectively, and money will find you.

The big shots are only the little shots who keep shooting.[12]

—Christopher Morley

As I mentioned earlier, Zig Ziglar says, "If you do more than you are paid to do, soon the day will come when you are paid more for what you do." I am a living witness of that. Pay the price for greatness, and you will reap the rewards. If you want to be successful, do what successful people do! Success leaves clues!

CHAPTER SUMMARY

EIGHT POINTS TO PONDER
DURING YOUR TRANSITION

1. Remember that there are three ways to get anything you want. First, identify the thing you want. Second, identify the price the thing you want will cost you. Third, pay the price.

2. Use your dream job to set up a very solid financial foundation for your dream, and keep multiple streams of income flowing into your life and business.

3. Your dream team consists of industry-specific mentors, CFP, CPA, and payroll specialist. They save you tons more money than they cost you.

4. Buy a nice home before you transition if you can. Let it appreciate in value, and if you need to, use the equity in the home to finance your dream yourself. Never let dollars delay your destiny. Find a workaround!

5. Give your dreams their own real identity with bank accounts, tax IDs, business cards, and so on. You and the general public will take your dreams more seriously this way.

6. Think big, start small, and scale fast!

7. Consider the many benefits that a network marketing company can provide you. It's an easy, low-cost way to see if you have what it takes to be an entrepreneur without much risk and with plenty of transferable learning that you can use in any industry.

8. Get around people who are doing what you want to do or are doing now but who are doing way better than you. Continue to learn from everything and everyone.

CONCLUSION

A journey of a thousand miles begins with a single step.
—Chinese Proverb

YOU DID IT! YOU FINISHED WHAT YOU STARTED, AND I AM BEYOND PROUD of you for that accomplishment. Just as experiencing this book has been a journey for you, writing it was a tremendous journey for me. However, the great thing is that we made it to the end, and we did it together. I once was where you are now. I once was caught, but now I am free, and that's ultimately what I want this book to do for you. I want it to help you become free. You know, in truth, I believe that freedom is one of the most profound causes for which people live, die, and make changes in their lives. We all want freedom— freedom to love, freedom to earn a living doing what we enjoy, freedom to afford nice things for our family and friends, freedom to worship and praise God, freedom to love whom we choose to love, freedom to live our purpose and maximize our potential, freedom to live in multicultural and multigenerational neighborhoods, freedom to laugh, freedom to cry, freedom to manifest all the things we think in our minds. The reason you have to leave your current job is because you need the freedom of a dream job to help you transition. But one day you will have to leave your dream job because you need and want the freedom to live your ultimate dreams full-time! The key to all of this is to passionately and strategically pursue the greatness that was entrusted to you at birth and impact as many lives as you can in the process. As you move forward from this book, please allow me to challenge you to do the following:

1. **Go back and reread this book** and complete the exercises. There is simply too much meat in this book for you to have picked it all up on the first go-around. Repetition is the mother of skill, so go back over this book, especially the chapters that gave you the most *aha* moments. Hopefully you participated actively with this book, and in doing so, you completed all the exercises that I gave you throughout the chapters. If you did, move on to the next challenge. However, if you did not and you simply read this book as fast as you could just to say you finished it, I applaud you for finishing, but I challenge you to go back and participate with me at a deeper level. This journey to your success is not a sprint; it's a marathon. Take your time and go back over the things you may have skipped over.

2. **Apply what you have learned** and take action on the many things you have written down. Throughout this book you have acquired a lot of information and knowledge—some new and some old information presented in a new or different way. Regardless of that, now that you have the knowledge, you must turn it into power through your action steps. Wanting it is not enough. Desire is important, but action is what produces results and the manifestation of your wants. So go out and start implementing one by one the many things you have committed to in this book. Reflect on all the things you have learned, and make a plan of action as to how you will implement this new knowledge that you have.

    Stay thirsty for knowledge and information related to your calling and dream. Read books and attend seminars by people who are a hundred times more successful than I am. Study under the best of the best, because you were created by the best to give this world your best! I would highly recommend that you hire a coach. Trained and/or certified coaches are the secret weapons of the super successful. A personal and/or professional coach will be a tremendous source of support, encouragement, and accountability for you as you move through your transition. Additionally, coaches are excellent strategic allies who will assist you in gaining clarity about your life and your ultimate dream occupation. Visit my Web site to learn more about various coaching resources that I recommend; also check out the informational page following this chapter to learn more about the many wonderful coaching opportunities that Delatorro Worldwide Empowerment has to offer.

3. **Send me an e-mail** to caught@delncneal.com and let me know how this book has changed your life. Most authors write books and never look back on the real difference that the book made in the lives of the people who read it. I want you to share with me how this book has impacted your life, your family, your business, and your destiny! Visit my Web site www.DelMcNeal.com and give me your feedback on the book.

4. **Share this book and its impact with others** whom you know and love. If this book has blessed your life in major ways, why keep it a secret? Tell your friends, family, co-workers, and neighbors. Form book clubs and special "Caught Between" empowerment groups to study the material at deeper levels. Encourage as many people as you can to go online or to their nearest bookstore to buy this book today!

Now that you have finished the book, start a new chapter in your life. Chapters are great because so many things can change from one chapter to the next. Just as you have experienced with this book and many other books you have read, each chapter held new discoveries, insights, pearls of wisdom, and strategies of success for your life. So go ahead and start a new chapter, because when the chapter changes, the characters can change. When the chapter changes, the plot can change. When the chapter changes, the focus can change. When the chapter changes, the entire ending can be altered. When the chapter changes, new characters can be introduced. When the chapter changes, answers can emerge where there once were only puzzling questions. So I challenge you to look at every major occurrence that happens in your life (good, bad, or indifferent) as an opportunity to close one chapter and start another. This conclusion commemorates your finishing this book, but in truth commencements are not the end of something but rather the beginning of something new. Just as I told you in the introduction of this book, mark today down on your calendar as the day that you started a brand-new chapter of your life story. You hold the pen in your hands. Write daily, and create your masterpiece!

It is my sincere prayer, hope, desire, and full expectation that this book has empowered you and will continue to challenge you to do just as it says: *leave your nine-to-five job behind and step into the life you've always wanted.* May the blessings and the favor of God be upon your every endeavor and destiny venture. Know that I am somewhere around the world believing in you! God bless.

NOTES

INTRODUCTION

1. Problems Quotes and Quotations Compiled by GIGA, http://www.giga-usa
   .com/quotes/topics/problems_t001.htm (accessed August 24, 2007).

CHAPTER 1
THERE IS A PLACE CALLED
"THERE"—IT'S CALLED *YOUR DESTINY*

1. ThinkExist.com, "Jack Welch Quotes," http://thinkexist.com/quotation/
   control_your_own_destiny_or_someone_else_will/151582.html (accessed
   September 28, 2007).

2. Stephen Covey, *The 7 Habits of Highly Effective People* (New York: Free Press,
   2004).

3. ThinkExist.com, "James A. Michener Quotes," http://thinkexist.com/
   quotation/the_master_in_the_art_of_living_makes_little/295791.html
   (accessed August 30, 2008).

4. Rick Warren, *The Purpose-Driven Life* (Grand Rapids, MI: Zondervan, 2002).

CHAPTER 2
WHOEVER TOLD YOU TO JOB?

1. Mark Twain, "A Humorist's Confession," *New York Times*, November 26, 1905,
   http://www.twainquotes.com/Work.html (accessed August 30, 2007).

2. ThinkExist.com, "Mahatma Gandhi Quotes," http://thinkexist.com/quotation/
   be_the_change_you_want_to_see_in_the_world/148490.html (accessed
   September 28, 2007).

3. Nido Qubein, keynote speech, 2006 NSA National Convention.

4. "Executives Reveal Their 'Dream Jobs' In BusinessWeek Research Services Career Survey," http://www.prnewswire.com/cgi-bin/stories .pl?ACCT=104&STORY=/www/story/08-10-2004/0002228787&EDATE (accessed September 4, 2007).

5. Scott Reeves, "Loving the Job You Hate," December 1, 2005, http://www .forbes.com/careers/2005/11/30/career-work-employment-cx_sr_ 1201bizbasics.html (accessed September 4, 2007).

6. "U.S. Job Satisfaction Declines, The Conference Board Reports," February 23, 2007, http://www.conference-board.org/economics/pressView.cfm?press_ ID=3075 (accessed September 4, 2007).

7. Rick Warren, *Growing Spiritually at Work*, Part 1 (audiocassette).

8. Steven Sauter et al, "Stress . . . at Work," National Institute for Occupational Health and Safety, http://www.cdc.gov/niosh/stresswk.html (accessed September 4, 2007).

9. CareerBuilder.com, "Four-in-Ten Workers Live Paycheck to Paycheck, According to CareerBuilder.com Survey" March 12, 2007, http://www. careerbuilder.com/share/aboutus/pressreleasesdetail.aspx?id=pr357&sd=3/12/ 2007&ed=12/31/2007&cbRecursionCnt=1&cbsid=42f667cb7b5642a0803cbe 8256c5afc2-242235112-WB-2&ns_siteid=ns_us_g_Many_US_workers_live__ (accessed September 20, 2007).

10. Arthur Miller Jr. with William Hendricks, *The Power of Uniqueness: How to Become Who You Really Are* (Grand Rapids, MI: Zondervan, 2002).

11. Nicholas Lore, *The Pathfinder: How to Choose or Change Your Career for a Lifetime of Satisfaction and Success* (New York: Simon and Schuster, 1998).

12. Ellen Galinsky, Stacy Kim, and James Bond, *Feeling Overworked: When Work Becomes Too Much* (New York, Family and Work Institute, 2001), http:// familiesandwork.org/site/research/summary/feelingoverworkedsumm.pdf (accessed September 4, 2007).

13. Salary.com, "Mind the Job Satisfaction Gap: HR Professionals Underestimate Intensity of Employee Job Searches and Employees Fall Victim to 'Grass Is Greener' Syndrome," http://www.salary.com/aboutus/layoutscripts/ abtl_default.asp?tab=abt&cat=cat012&ser=ser041&part=Par591&isdefault=0 (accessed September 4, 2007).

14. Ibid.

15. Ibid.

16. Ibid.

17. Ibid.

18. Rick Warren, *Growing Spiritually at Work*, Part 1 (audiocassette).

19. "U.S. Job Satisfaction Declines, The Conference Board Reports," February 23, 2007, http://www.conference-board.org/economics/pressView.cfm?press_ID=3075 (accessed September 4, 2007).

20. TheQuotationsPage.com, Johnny Carson, http://www.quotationspage.com/quotes/Johnny_Carson/ (accessed September 5, 2007).

21. *BusinessWeek* magazine online, http://www.businessweek.com/magazine/content/06_38/b4001848.htm?chan=smallbiz_sprb_u25

22. Roger Martin, "The Creative Age," *Rotman* magazine, Spring/Summer 2006, http://www.rotman.utoronto.ca/pdf/Rotman_spring06.pdf (accessed September 5, 2007).

23. Wikipedia.org, "Information Age," http://en.wikipedia.org/wiki/Information_age (accessed September 28, 2007).

24. Wikipedia.org, "Information Age."

25. Wikiquote.org, "Napolean Hill," http://en.wikiquote.org/wiki/Napoleon_Hill (accessed September 5, 2007).

26. ThinkExist.com, "James Allen Quotes," http://www.thinkexist.com/English/Author/x/Author_3200_1.htm (accessed September 5, 2007).

27. Mark Scharenbroich, speech at 2005 NSA National Convention.

28. BrainyQuote.com, "Thomas A. Edison Quotes," http://www.brainyquote.com/quotes/quotes/t/thomasaed109928.html (accessed September 5, 2007).

29. BrainyQuote.com, "Theodore Roosevelt Quotes," http://www.brainyquote.com/quotes/quotes/t/theodorero386123.html (accessed September 5, 2007).

30. ThinkExist.com, "Elbert Hubbard Quotes," http://thinkexist.com/quotation/we_work_to_become-not_to_acquire/144484.html (accessed September 5, 2007).

31. Robert Kiyosaki, *Rich Dad's Guide to Wealth With Robert Kiyosaki: A Look at How to Get Ahead Financially*, PBS, March 4, 2007.

32. JournalStar.com, Deena Winter, *Financial Planners: Winning the Lottery Isn't Always a Dream*, February 25, 2006, http://www.journalstar.com/articles/2006/02/25/special/doc4400ffe394163444263790.txt (accessed September 28, 2007).

33. The Mayo Clinic Staff, "Job satisfaction: Strategies to make work more gratifying," Mayoclinic.com, September 29, 2006, http://www.mayoclinic.com/health/job-satisfaction/WL00051 (accessed September 5, 2007).

34. ThinkExist.com, "W. M. Lewis Quotes," http://thinkexist.com/quotation/the_tragedy_of_life_is_not_that_it_ends_so_soon/227662.html (accessed September 5, 2007).

35. Anthony Robbins, "New Lens" lecture, Technology, Entertainment, and Design Conference, Monterey, CA, February 24, 2006.

36. Donald Trump and Robert Kiyosaki, *Why We Want You to Be Rich* (N.p.: Rich Press, 2006).

37. Michael Sasso, "Colleges Fight Job Offshoring," *Tampa Tribune*, http://www.redorbit.com/news/technology/898797/colleges_fight_job_offshoring/index.html (accessed September 6, 2007).

38. Alan Blinder, "How Many Jobs Might Be Offshoreable?" CEPS Working Paper No. 142, Princeton University, March 2007, http://www.princeton.edu/~ceps/workingpapers/142blinder.pdf (accessed September 6, 2007).

39. Kiyosaki, *Rich Dad, Poor Dad* (N.p.: Business Plus, 2000).

40. Steve Sjuggerud, *"Wealth Statistics: How Do You Measure Up vs. the "Average Wealthy American?,"* The Investment U E-Letter, Issue # 208, January 27, 2003, http://www.investmentu.com/IUEL/2003/20030127.html (accessed September 6, 2007).

41. Freedom Writers Foundation, "About Erin Gruwell," http://www.freedomwritersfoundation.org/site/c.kqIXL2PFJtH/b.2286935/k.AD6E/About_Erin_Gruwell.htm (accessed September 24, 2007).

42. American Program Bureau, "Inspirational Education/Catalyst for Social Change," biographical information on Erin Gruwell, http://www.apbspeakers.com/themes/defaultview/site/index.aspx (accessed September 27, 2008).

43. Earl Nightingale, *The Strangest Secret*, December 23, 1999, compact disc, The Keys Company, Inc.

CHAPTER 3
MY STORY: A LIFE BY DESIGN

1. Quotations.com, "Hal Lancaster," http://www.quotationspage.com/quote/25862.html (accessed September 6, 2007).

2. Willie Jolley, *It Only Takes a Minute to Change Your Life* (N.p., St. Martin's Press, 1997).

3. WhatQuote.com, "Peter F. Drucker Quotes," http://www.whatquote.com/ quotes/Peter-F--Drucker/31616-The-best-way-to-pred.htm (accessed September 7, 2007).

4. Robert Anthony, The Secret of Deliberate Creation, http://www. thesecretofdeliberatecreation.com/ (accessed September 7, 2007).

5. ThinkExist.com, "Saint Augustine Quotes," http://thinkexist.com/quotation/ pray_as_though_everything_depended_on_god-work_as/149654.html (accessed September 24, 2007).

6. ThinkExist.com, "Jim Rohn Quotes," http://thinkexist.com/quotation/we-must-all-suffer-from-one-of-two-pains-the-pain/347821.html (accessed Spetember 7, 2007).

7. Mike Murdock, Keynote speech, Wisdom Breakfast 2003, Marriott Hotel, Tampa, Florida.

8. ThinkExist.com, "Kahlil Gibran Quotes," http://thinkexist.com/quotation/ faith_is_a_knowledge_within_the_heart-beyond_the/148221.html (accessed September 10, 2007).

9. *The Karate Kid, Part III*, "Memorable Quotes," http://www.imdb.com/title/ tt0097647/quotes (accessed September 10, 2007).

CHAPTER 4
YOUR LIFE'S PURPOSE:
THE CATALYST TO YOUR DREAMS

1. BrainyQuote.com, "Robert Byrne Quotes," http://www.brainyquote.com/ quotes/quotes/r/robertbyrn101054.html (accessed September 10, 2007).

2. Abundance-and-Happiness.com, "Purpose Quotes," http://www.abundance-and-happiness.com/purpose-quotes.html (accessed September 10, 2007).

3. *The 7 Habits of Highly Effective People* Online Discussion Guide, Habit 2: "Begin with the End in Mind: Principles of Personal Leadership," http://www.leaderu. com/cl-institute/habits/habit2.html (accessed September 10, 2007).

4. Tony McGee, *Can't Shove a Great Life Into a Small Dream* (Woodland Hills, CA: Platinum Star Publishing, n.d.).

5. Mike Murdock, *101 Wisdom Keys* (N.p., Wisdom International, 2004).

CHAPTER 5
THE ICEBERG THEORY:
UTILIZING YOUR OCCUPATION TO EXPLODE YOUR POTENTIAL

1. QuoteWorld.com, "Ralph Waldo Emerson," http://www.quoteworld.org/quotes/4458 (accessed September 24, 2007).

2. Abundance-and-Happiness.com, "Potential Quotes," http://www.abundance-and-happiness.com/potential-quotes.html (accessed September 11, 2007).

3. ThinkExist.com, "Wilma Rudolph Quotes," http://thinkexist.com/quotation/never_underestimate_the_power_of_dreams_and_the/15261.html (accessed September 12, 2007).

4. Abundance-and-Happiness.com, "Potential Quotes," http://www.abundance-and-happiness.com/potential-quotes.html (accessed September 12, 2007).

5. Brian Tracy, *Goals!: How to Get Everything You Want—Faster Than You Ever Thought Possible* (N.p.: Berrett-Koehler Publishers, 2003), http://books.google.com/books?id=psJSzql5bxEC&pg=PA7&lpg=PA7&dq=the+potential+of+the+average+person+is+like+a+huge+ocean+unsailed+a+new+continent+unexplored&source=web&ots=Ciqjq4dTb4&sig=KjqKJMbBK14NSnX77fwYrHr6a_s#PPA7,M1 (accessed September 12, 2007).

6. Kiyowsaki, *Rich Dad, Poor Dad.*

7. QuoteWorld.com, "Anne Frank," http://www.quoteworld.org/quotes/4908 (accessed September 12, 2007).

8. Abundance-and-Happiness.com, "Potential Quotes," http://www.abundance-and-happiness.com/potential-quotes.html (accessed September 12, 2007).

9. Les Brown, *It's Not Over Until You Win*, five compact discs.

10. Gary Coxe, *Secrets That My Millionare Mentors Taught Me About Business and Success*, six compact discs.

11. QuotationsPage.com, "Cole's Quotables," http://www.quotationspage.com/quote/5049.html (accessed September 13, 2007).

12. The Quotations and Sayings Database, "Difference," http://www.quotesandsayings.com/gdifference.htm (accessed September 13, 2007).

13. ThinkExist.com, "Bill Bradley Quotes," http://thinkexist.com/quotation/leadership_is_unlocking_people-s_potential_to/151085.html (accessed September 13, 2007).

CHAPTER 6
IT'S TIME TO TRANSITION

1. ThinkExist.com, "David Viscott Quotes," http://thinkexist.com/quotation/ the_only_thing_that_stands_between_a_man_and_what/203442.html (accessed September 13, 2007).

2. BrainyQuote.com, "Denis Waitley Quotes," http://www.brainyquote.com/ quotes/authors/d/denis_waitley.html (accessed September 13, 2007).

3. ThinkExist.com, "Napolean Hill Quotes," http://thinkexist.com/quotation/ don-t_wait-the_time_will_never_be_just_right/294621.html (accessed September 13, 2007).

4. BrainyQuote.com, "Jim Rohn Quotes," http://www.brainyquote.com/quotes/ authors/j/jim_rohn.html (accessed September 13, 2007).

5. ThinkExist.com, "Mark Twain Quotes," http://thinkexist.com/quotation/ twenty_years_from_now_you_will_be_more/215220.html (accessed September 13, 2007).

CHAPTER 7
HARNESSING THE POWER OF THE DREAM JOB

1. BrainyQuote.com, "Jesse Jackson Quotes," http://www.brainyquote.com/ quotes/quotes/j/jessejacks130038.html (accessed September 13, 2007).

2. ThinkExist.COM, "George Bernard Shaw," http://thinkexist.com/quotation/ people_are_always_blaming_their_circumstances_for/155215.html (accessed September 14, 2007).

3. Katherine Hansen, *A Foot in the Door: Networking Your Way Into the Hidden Job Market* (N.p.: Ten Speed Press, 2000).

4. ThinkExist.com, "Victor Hugo Quotes," http://thinkexist.com/quotation/ there_is_nothing_like_a_dream_to_create_the/145393.html (accessed September 14, 2007).

CHAPTER 8
ATTITUDE TIPS

1. Brian Tracy, *Time Power: A Proven System for Getting More Done in Less Time Than You Ever Thought Possible* (N.p.: AMACOM/American Management Association, 2004), 27.

2. ThinkExist.com, "Scott Hamilton Quotes," http://thinkexist.com/quotation/the_only_disability_in_life_is_a_bad_attitude/219108.html (accessed September 13, 2007).

3. Jack Loechner, *"TV's Turned On Eight Hours a Day; Average Person Watches Four and a Half Hours,"* Research Brief from the Center for Media Research, October 21, 2005, http://publications.mediapost.com/index.cfm?fuseaction=Articles.showArticle&art_aid=35192 (accessed September 13, 2007).

4. Thomas J. Stanley and William D. Danko, *The Millionaire Next Door*, (N.p.: Pocket Books, 1998).

5. Keith Harrell, *Attitude Is Everything: 10 Life-Changing Steps to Turning Attitude Into Action* (N.p: Collins, 2000).

6. Dennis Mannering and Wendy Mannering, *Attitudes Are Contagious: Are Yours Worth Catching?* (N.p.: Options Unlimited, Inc., 1986).

CHAPTER 9
SPIRITUAL AND EMOTIONAL TIPS

1. ThinkExist.com, "Marshal Ferdinand Foch Quotes," http://thinkexist.com/quotation/the_most_powerful_weapon_on_earth_is_the_human/216171.html (accessed September 13, 2007).

2. BrainyQuote.com, "M. Scott Peck Quotes," http://www.brainyquote.com/quotes/quotes/m/mscottpec160096.html (accessed September 13, 2007).

3. Anthony Robbins, *Personal Power II*, compact disc.

4. ThinkExist.com, "George Bernard Shaw Quotes," http://thinkexist.com/quotation/we_don-t_stop_playing_because_we_grow_old-we_grow/13470.html (accessed September 14, 2007).

5. About.com: Quotes, "Inspirational Problem-Solving Quotes," http://quotations.about.com/cs/inspirationquotes/a/ProblemSolvi1.htm (accessed September 14, 2007).

6. BrainyQuote.com, "Wayne Dyer Quotes," http://www.brainyquote.com/quotes/quotes/w/waynedyer133317.html (accessed September 14, 2007).

CHAPTER 10
SOCIAL AND RELATIONAL TIPS

1. BrainyQuote.com, "Theodore Roosevelt Quotes," http://www.brainyquote.com/quotes/quotes/t/theodorero122116.html (accessed September 14, 2007).

2. Jeffrey Gitomer, *Little Black Book of Connections* (Austin, TX: Bard Press, 2006).

3. Ibid.

4. Napolean Hill, *Think and Grow Rich* (N.p.: Aventine Press, 2004).

5. Murdock, *101 Wisdom Keys*.

6. Mike Murdock, *The Law of Recognition* (N.p.: Wisdom International, 1999).

7. Gitomer, *Little Black Book of Connections*.

CHAPTER 11
TIME MASTERY TIPS

1. Zig Ziglar, *Over the Top*, compact discs.

2. Murdock, *101 Wisdom Keys*.

3. John Maxwell, *Today Matters* (N.p.: Center Street, 2005).

4. BrainyQuote.com, "Samuel Smiles Quotes," http://www.brainyquote.com/quotes/quotes/s/samuelsmil155135.html (accessed September 14, 2007).

5. BrainyQuote.com, "Robert Orben Quotes," http://www.brainyquote.com/quotes/authors/r/robert_orben.html (accessed September 14, 2007).

CHAPTER 12
FINANCIAL AND ENTREPRENEURIAL TIPS

1. Scott Allen, "Quotations From Famous Entrepreneurs on Entrepreneurship," About.com, http://entrepreneurs.about.com/od/famousentrepreneurs/a/quotations.htm (accessed September 14, 2007).

2. Robert Kiyosaki, *How to Get Rich Without Cutting Up Your Credit Cards*, compact discs.

3. ThinkExist.com, "Oprah Winfrey Quotes," http://thinkexist.com/quotation/passion_is_energy-feel_the_power_that_comes_from/341206.html (accessed September 14, 2007).

4. BrainyQuote.com, "Norman Vincent Peale," http://www.brainyquote.com/quotes/quotes/n/normanvinc106832.html (accessed September 14, 2007).

5. Robert Allen, *Multiple Streams of Income* (N.p.: Wiley, 2005).

6. Harold Myra and Marshal Shelley, *The Leadership Secrets of Billy Graham* (Grand Rapids, MI: Zondervan, 2005), 118.

7. *Forbes* magazine, "The Richest People in the World," Billionaire Special Issue, March 27, 2006.

8. BrainyQuote.com, "Oprah Winfrey Quotes," http://www.brainyquote.com/quotes/quotes/o/oprahwinfr173384.html (accessed September 14, 2007).

9. World-of-Quotes.com, "Science and Technology Quotes," http://www.worldofquotes.com/topic/Science-and-Technology/1/index.html (accessed September 14, 2007).

10. Scott Allen, "Quotations from Famous Entrepreneurs on Entrepreneurship," About.com, http://entrepreneurs.about.com/od/famousentrepreneurs/a/quotations.htm (accessed September 14, 2007).

11. ThinkExist.com, "Ayn Rand Quotes," http://thinkexist.com/quotation/wealth_is_the_product_of_man-s_capacity_to_think/220796.html (accessed September 14, 2007).

12. BrainyQuote.com, "Christopher Morley Quotes," http://www.brainyquote.com/quotes/authors/c/christopher_morley.html (accessed September 14, 2007).